The 4:2 Formula®

| GETTING BUYERS OFF THE FENCE AND INTO A HOME |

JEFF SHORE

10th ANNIVERSARY EDITION
UPDATED AND EXPANDED

ISBN: 978-0-9884915-9-5

Copyright 2023 by Jeff Shore and Shore Consulting, Inc.

All rights reserved. Printed in the United States of America. Except as permitted under the United States Copyright Act of 1976, no part of this publication may be reproduced or distributed in any form or by any means, or stored in a database or retrieval system, without the prior written permission of the publisher.

Cover and page design by Six Penny Graphics.

Shore Consulting books are available at special quantity discounts to use as premiums and sales promotions or for use in corporate training programs. To contact a representative, please visit the Contact page at www.jeffshore.com or call +1 844-54-SHORE.

Table of Contents

About Jeff Shore. vii
The 4:2 Formula®: Getting Started ix

Section 1:
The Clients' Mission

1   Why Do People Move? 3
2   Understanding Dissatisfaction 11
3   Types and Degrees of Dissatisfaction 19
4   The Power of "Why?". 27
5   The Why Behind the "Why?". 33
6   Boldness in Questioning 41

Section 2:
The Formula for Change

7   Motivation Factor #1: Current Dissatisfaction . . . 49
8   Motivation Factor #2: Future Promise 57
9   Inhibitor Factor #1: Cost 67
10 Inhibitor Factor #2: Fear 73
11 The Buying Formula™ 81

Section 3:
The Sales 4:2 Formula

12	Scripting the Presentation	97
13	Why vs. What	105
14	The 4:2 Formula® Progression	111
15	Discovery Category #1: Relationship Building . .	117
16	Discovery Category #2: Motivation Questions . . .	127
17	Discovery Category #3: Current Dissatisfaction . .	135
18	Discovery Category #4: Future Promise	141
19	The Vision Agreements	149
20	Summary Question #1: The Summary Dissatisfaction Question (SDQ)	153
21	Summary Question #2: The Summary Solution Question (SSQ)	159
22	Filling In the Information Gaps	165

Section 4:
Implementation

The 10-Week Study Guide to 4:2 Selling. 175
Success Stories 193
Sample Scripts. 201

Dedicated to Amy O'Connor. I gave birth to the 4:2 Formula. Amy raised it, perfected it, and made it what it is today. The entire homebuilding industry owes her a debt of thanks.

About Jeff Shore

Jeff is the Founder of Shore Consulting, Inc., a company specializing in field-tested and proven psychology-based sales training programs for the real estate industry. Jeff is a top-selling author and an award-winning keynote speaker. He holds the prestigious Certified Speaking Professional designation from the National Speakers Association and is a member of the NSA's exclusive Million Dollar Speakers Group.

With over 30 years of real-world, frontline experience, Jeff's advanced sales strategies spring from extensive research into the psychology of buying and selling. He teaches salespeople how to climb inside the minds of their customers to sell the way their buyers want to buy. Using these modern, game-changing techniques, Jeff Shore's clients generated over $54 billion in sales last year.

linkedin.com/in/jeffshore

The 4:2 Formula®: Getting Started

I'd like to make a slightly preposterous claim: If you know your clients well enough, they will show you how to sell them a home. I believe this because I've seen it work over and over again, all around the world.

I also suggest that one of the biggest problems salespeople face is having been taught an approach that centers on the product rather than on the prospect. All too often, the sales presentation is nothing more than a massive assault of features and benefits. It's as if the salesperson is saying, "Open wide while I jam this down your throat. Then you can tell me if you like the taste."

At the core of this issue is a lack of understanding about why our clients are standing in front of us in the first place. We'll dive into that issue in this book. Sure, we want to know how to lure prospects off the fence, but shouldn't we first want to know what got them on the fence in the first place? We'll tackle that one as well. As salespeople, we want to get to the specifics of the home search, but we often stop short of understanding why those specifics *mean* something to a particular buyer. Yep, that's on the list as well.

In the pages that follow, I'd like to help you understand your clients at a level you've never thought possible. In doing so, I'll show you how to establish a sense of mutual purpose—a connection that puts you shoulder to shoulder with your client as you walk down the sales path. In the process, I'd like to help you become that trusted advisor you aspire to be.

Now, let me tell you what you *won't* find in this book.

First, you won't find pages and pages of scripts to memorize. Yes, there are samples of phrasings, but I leave it up to you to find and use your own sales voice.

Second, you won't find a lot of outrageous and unusable sales lines. I believe that salespeople serve through *leading* their clients, not through *manipulating* them.

Third, you won't find a lot of stories about the way the author used to do things in 1985. This book is relevant and timely for today; the principles are being applied all over the world every single day.

Fourth and finally, you won't find the "same old thing" in these pages. Instead, you'll discover a unique approach to getting to know your clients on a deep level. You'll notice a stark absence of questions like these: "How many bedrooms are you looking for?"; "What brought you out today?"; "How soon are you thinking about moving?"; and "What's your price range?"

My role in writing this book is to bring you fresh new concepts that can completely revolutionize your sales process. You have a part as well, and it begins with *active reading*. That's why I encourage you—I *beg* you—to read each chapter with a pen, notebook, and highlighter. Stop frequently and jot down your thoughts and highlight key concepts. Write out phrasing for your own sales language. Challenge yourself to practice out loud as you go along (unless you're reading this book at the library!).

As an added challenge, consider sending me a photograph of your extremely marked-up book. It always brings a joy to my heart when I see a book full of dog-eared pages, post-it notes, and highlighted text. Send me a pic, please! (jeff@jeffshore.com)

To support you in your journey, you'll find Application Breaks throughout the book. These are tips and ideas you can use repeatedly. That way, you aren't only gaining an intellectual understanding; you're also honing specific skills. You will also find Study Questions at the end of each chapter. Don't skip over these! They'll help you apply what you're learning as you go.

I *know* you can get a great deal out of the concepts that follow. But this book wasn't written for you to get something out of it; it was written to get something out of you—*your very best sales presentation!*

Let's do it. Let's change someone's world today!

SECTION 1:

◆ ◆ ◆

The Clients' Mission

Chapter One

Why Do People Move?

> *"If you know your customer well enough, the sales path will roll out in front of you."*
> – Jeff Shore

What is the single most motivating factor in a home-buying decision?

Think about your typical clients for a moment. Maybe they're young couples just buying their first home, ready to start a family and live the American dream. They've spent the past few years moving from one crappy apartment to the next as they get their careers off the ground. Now, they're looking for the perfect home.

Or perhaps your typical clients are middle-aged couples. They've recently sent the last of their brood off to college and have suddenly realized the family home is too big for just two. Besides, they want to live closer to the city where the restaurants are. They would love to have a luxury condo as a base camp for their upcoming travels and adventures.

Perhaps it's the multi-generational family moving in together. Or the single woman, career-minded and driven. Or the relocation buyer moving from out of state to your city.

Question: What do these clients have in common?

Your instinctive answer is that they're looking for the perfect home. Or perhaps you think the decision is about convenience, a good neighborhood, great location, or the alluring features and amenities a home has to offer. Maybe you suggest that they're seeking the home of their dreams and once they see it, they'll fall in love and just have to buy it. And of course, everyone will live happily ever after, right?

But that wasn't the question.

Again, the real question is "What is the single most motivating factor in a home-buying decision?"

The fact is this: Location, convenience, neighborhood, and even the features of a home are all things that might cause a client to buy one home over the other. But that's not the single most motivating factor in a home-buying decision. It goes much deeper.

Take a moment to get into your client's head on this one. Go ahead, I'll wait…

Do you know the single most motivating factor? In a word: Dissatisfaction.

That's probably not what you expected to hear, but if you understand this as part of the homebuyer's mindset, you will have a significant leg up on your competitors. You will learn things about your clients that most salespeople will never know. And the sale will roll out right in front of you.

Let's explore this idea in more depth.

Think about the home *you* are living in right now. Then rate your dissatisfaction with that home. On a scale of 1 to 10, with 1 meaning that you're very happy with the home, the neighborhood, and so on. It's your dream home, and you wouldn't even think about living anywhere else.

At the other end of the scale, a rating of 10 means you're highly dissatisfied, perhaps the neighborhood has been in steady decline, the basement floods with the slightest bit of rain, the neighbors play polka music at ungodly hours, and you just can't bear to stay another night in the place!

Where does your home rate on the scale?

Let's assume you're in the majority, which is 4 or below. You're fairly satisfied and have very few issues, if any at all, about your current living situation. It would be safe to say your discontent level is low. So, how would your home search be coming along right now? You would be actively looking, wouldn't you? No?

Of course not! You see, people who have little dissatisfaction with their homes are not in the market. In fact, they aren't even lookers. I could show that kind of client the nicest, most tricked-out home in town. It's got quartz countertops, top-of-the-line appliances, and a huge soaking tub. It's been decked out by one of the top designers in town; it's located in a gated community with just the sweetest neighbors I could find…all at a 10% discount. Sounds like a winner, right?

But if you're 100% satisfied with the home you live in now, *all those things don't matter.*

> "The 'why' is what brings the buyer through the doors. Buyers don't come looking to make a change as big as buying a new home because of a 'what'; they come because of their 'why.' They're trying to improve their life by changing something that's not working. The 4:2 Formula helps us figure out what it is that isn't working!"
> —Chris Brazeal, New Home Sales Manager

Dissatisfaction-Motivation Relationship

I contend that the single most motivating factor in buying a home is dissatisfaction. It also happens to be one of the most under-discovered aspects of the selling process.

Application Break

- Take time right now to evaluate your opening questions. Think about what you typically ask your clients when you first meet—that is, after you say "hello" but before you start talking about what you'd like to show them.

- Do those early questions lead you to a deep sense of what is wrong with their lives, and with how their lives need to be improved? Do the questions address what the clients are moving toward, or about what they're moving away from?

- Be thinking about the questions you could be asking to determine that sense of dissatisfaction.

Dismantling the Critical Path

If you've been in the real estate industry for any length of time, you've probably come across this "Critical Path" sales method: Greet, qualify, demonstrate, close. It seems as if every sales guru in the real estate industry has a variation of the Critical Path method—one that's guaranteed to make you a top producer.

If only it were that easy! I'm here to refute that method. I'm simply not a Critical Path guy...never have been and never will be.

You see, your clients don't operate in a vacuum. They can't be fenced in by a method that doesn't allow for one of the most important factors of selling: that you're dealing with human beings *who operate on emotion*. The problem with the Critical Path method is that it's both linear and overly simplistic. More important, it's about how the seller wants to sell.

Let's talk instead about *how the buyer wants to buy*.

RYAN TAFT
Mastery Level Insights

Imagine for a moment that you're having a coffee with a friend, and you ask what they've been up to. The friend replies, *"It looks like I'm going to have to move."* What would be your response? Would it be: *"How many bedrooms are you looking for?"* or *"What's your time frame?"* or *"Are you working with a Realtor?"*

Probably not. My guess is you would ask, *"Why?"* In other words, you would be a human being. Unfortunately, that's not what most salespeople do.

Have you ever seen a couple pull into your community and sit in the car for a minute or two before coming into your sales office? Do you know what they were doing in the car? If you

> guessed game-planning, you'd be right. They were strategizing how to get away from you. But why? Why are so many customers so leery of salespeople?
>
> I believe that too many buyers have been subjected to a slew of salespeople who use scripted, predictable questions via the critical path. The questions are product-centered and not customer-centered. Honestly, it feels more like an interrogation than a sales conversation!
>
> Salespeople who follow the Critical Path are all too often focused on their commission. With the 4:2 Formula, you're focused on the *customer's mission*.

Sure, you can greet your clients, find out how much house they can afford, and proceed to show them home after home after home. At that rate, you'll be spinning your wheels trying to get those clients to make a purchase decision. That is, if they don't just jump ship before then and find someone who actually understands them!

So, let's not concern ourselves with methods designed to help the seller sell right now. When dealing with homebuyers, I'm far more interested in how the buyers will buy and what drives their choice. What motivates people to pull the trigger and happily sign on the dotted line?

In fact, I'll repeat what I said in the introduction to this book: "If you know your clients well enough, they will show you how to sell them a home. If you truly understand them on a deep enough level, the sales path should roll right out in front of you."

And believe me; it will. At that point, your clients will roll out the red carpet of their innermost hopes, fears, and dreams. However, being able to reach this point requires a greater sense of partnership than ever. And that partnership is dependent upon trust and a deep sense of insight into the dissatisfaction they're feeling.

> **Winning Thought:** Let the sales path appear as you get to know your client's deepest motivations.

Study Questions

1. What did you learn about why people move?

2. What is the single most motivating factor in a home-buying decision?

3. What was your personal motivating factor in your last home-buying decision? How did this tie to dissatisfaction?

4. The "Critical Path" sales method says "greet, qualify, demonstrate, close." Why is this approach ineffective in selling a house?

5. Why is it so important to understand *why* an individual homebuyer wants to buy?

Chapter Two

Understanding Dissatisfaction

> The "why" is far more important than the "what."

During her junior year of college, my daughter Katie came home for Mother's Day weekend, driving 400 miles from Southern to Northern California. Katie's glamorous ride was actually my old pickup truck that I lent her to have at school.

At nine o'clock in the evening on the Thursday before Mother's Day, she called me on her cell phone from a loud place; that turned out to be the shoulder of Interstate 80. My truck had simply stopped running. Please understand the context: This is not a call a father likes to receive. I didn't like the idea of Katie being stranded like that.

We had the truck towed to our mechanic who called me Friday afternoon to officially pronounce the old pickup—in mechanical terms—dead. A blown head gasket had torn apart the radiator, which damaged one thing and then the other thing…you get the picture.

That call came in late on Friday. Katie was leaving for Southern California after church on Sunday. First question: What did our Saturday plans now consist of? If your answer was "car shopping," you would be wrong. We were not car *shopping*; we were car *buying!*

Next question: How important was my little story for the salesperson at the car dealership? One would think it to be critical. Yet we went to three different dealerships and not one salesperson figured it out. No one asked about our situation, about our story. What do you think they wanted to talk about? You got it—prices. Terms. Discounts. Incentives.

> **Ignore the dissatisfaction and you will frustrate the entire sales process.**

As you can see, dissatisfaction can be a powerful motivator. Without it, we might be tempted to put off what *must* get done. Dissatisfaction provides us with the desire to change our situation. *This is as true in life as it is in sales.* Have you ever been so hungry that you've surprised yourself with what you were willing to eat?

Say you have a big meeting at work and decide to skip lunch one day. You might feel a bit hungry, but it really isn't a pressing matter, and you're able to hold off until dinner with no sweat. Imagine though, that you've gone 24 hours without food. The urgency to eat becomes stronger and, instead of reaching for your usual healthy meal, you pull into a drive-through and get the greasiest burger they sell. Probably not the best option, but hey—you were hungry.

Now, imagine yourself out in the wilderness. You haven't eaten in four days. You're lightheaded, irritable, sluggish, and your stomach feels like it's eating itself. You see a cicada latched onto a tree, and suddenly something you never thought you

Understanding Dissatisfaction

would eat looks incredibly scrumptious. You're ravished, so you pick it off and eat it. At this point, you'll do anything to quell the ache in your empty stomach.

In this situation, your hunger acts as a motivator for change, and you'll do anything to make that change happen and the hunger feelings go away. You'll even do things you may not have considered before.

That's dissatisfaction.

> **Dissatisfaction is the driving force behind urgency.**

In the decision to move, there's no more powerful factor than dissatisfaction. But wait—it gets better because not only does dissatisfaction prove to be a powerful motivator; dissatisfaction is also the driving force behind urgency. Just like the urgency experienced by the person who hasn't eaten in days, clients who are dissatisfied with their home have that same emotional thought pattern. They need to move, *and* they needed to make it happen yesterday.

Let me put that another way. The higher the dissatisfaction, the greater the urgency. If you can answer the call of their urgent pleas, you will be their hero.

In my work with real estate companies around the world, I'm constantly hit with the same question: "How come we can't get these buyers off the fence?" That's a good question, but I have a better one: "What got them on the fence in the first place?"

Figure out what got them on the fence, and you'll figure out how to get them off the fence. If you've ever wondered what makes homebuyers get off the fence, start with their dissatisfaction.

> **Application Break**
>
> - In your typical discovery process, how soon do you determine what got your clients on the fence? Do you learn it in the first few minutes, or does it seem to take significantly longer than that?
>
> - By now, you should be thinking about questions you could ask that would give you a deeper understanding of the client's dissatisfaction. Now begin to think about how to ask those questions early in the conversation. The sooner you know their pain, the sooner you can provide relief for it.

I don't suppose I'll ever become famous for this quote, but let me give it a try. *"The greatest motivation to buy new shoes is when you notice your sock is wet."*

No? Not exactly Covey-esque, is it? But the principle behind it is critically important.

It happened to me on a business trip to Chicago in January. I noticed my foot felt squishy, so I looked at the sole of my shoe and sure enough, a hole. Because I was on day two of a five-day trip, I had no choice; I had to buy a new pair of shoes.

Interestingly—and at a measure of surprise to me—I ended up buying the most expensive pair of shoes I've ever owned. The salesperson at Nordstrom already knew I needed to buy a pair of shoes; that was a given. But in his questioning, he discovered several things about me:

1. I am on my feet all day long; comfort is critical.

2. I want to project an image of success; cheap doesn't work.

3. I wear a lot of suits; an upscale oxford lace-up makes sense.

4. I'm constantly going through security at airports; it's a pain when it comes to removing my shoes.

He proceeded to show me a shoe that was stunningly classy and exceedingly comfortable. It had a hidden elastic in the side so it had the elegance of a lace-up but performed like a loafer—I could easily slip it on and off at an airport security line.

Only after I was absolutely sold did he share with me the price. *Did you catch that?* Only after I was absolutely sold did he share with me the price. When the dissatisfaction is high enough, and the future promise is great enough, the cost is practically a non-issue. Had he led the discussion with "What is your price range?" I would have purchased the wrong shoes!

If you remember nothing else from this book, remember this: **The single greatest force in a homebuyer's urgency is dissatisfaction.** This is because dissatisfaction causes us to feel uncomfortable, which creates the urgency *and* motivation to remove the source of that discomfort. The longer we go without being able to remove the discomfort and get back to a positive state of being, the more urgent our situation becomes. Sometimes, the urgency gets to the point of being willing to make pretty serious sacrifices to achieve a state of satisfaction once again.

MICHELLE BENDIEN
Mastery Level Insights

Industry-wide we often fail to realize that for our customers it's not about bedrooms or bathrooms or square footage or the purchase price. It isn't about any of those things – *unless* we make it about those things by customizing the conversation to the customer's Current Dissatisfaction.

Your customer is on a mission to improve their life. Something is not working for them, and they want it fixed. That dissatisfaction is a powerful motivator that is fueled by emotion. Whatever the issue, it was a big enough deal to get your customers off their couch, into their car, and into your sales center to see you. Understanding dissatisfaction is a critical component in the sales process that will help lead you and your customers to the *right* home. After all, how would you even know what right looks like if you don't first understand what wrong looks like?

So, it can be said that the higher the degree of dissatisfaction the homebuyers have, the higher their urgency is. Conversely, the lower the dissatisfaction they have, the less urgency they will have to make a change, if at all. That being said, there are different degrees or categories we can put this dissatisfaction into.

Let's take a look at that in the next chapter.

> *"Only after learning a buyer's 'why' does a salesperson really know which home to show the buyer. Sure, we have plenty of different floor plans and options, but none of it matters unless we TRULY understand WHY they're moving in the first place."*
> —Bryan DeGabrielle, Vice President of Sales

Study Questions

1. Think back to a time you had your own "squishy foot" experience and had to buy something urgently. What was it? How did you decide what to buy? How did you feel about your decision?

2. How can you use personal understanding to help you look for urgency factors from your clients *and* help them be ready to make a decision to buy?

3. Do you have the patience to spend time understanding your clients' Current Dissatisfaction? If not, what can you do to increase your patience?

4. Think about your last two or three home-buying clients. List some of their underlying needs—ones that would help them be sold on a property *before* you bring up price.

Chapter Three

Types and Degrees of Dissatisfaction

> *"He who has a why to live can bear almost any how."*
> – Nietzsche

Dissatisfaction comes in many forms; there are numerous reasons why homebuyers might feel the urgency to move. At times, that dissatisfaction might be tied to the home itself, but it could also be about other things. For some homebuyers, dissatisfaction originates with a life change, such as a new job, getting married, or having a baby. All of these changes can cause homebuyers to assess whether their current home will meet their needs of the future. If it won't, they'll likely become dissatisfied and feel the need to find something more suitable.

So, what pushes those clients over the edge and makes them say, "This is it! I'm not putting up with this leaking roof, polka-playing neighbors, and downtrodden neighborhood. It's time to move on and find something better!"

Think about it for a moment. Why couldn't they stay where they were and just, you know, make it work? What was it about their lives that needed to improve?

In some cases, the answer is simple. Maybe one of them got a new job out of state. Maybe they had the perfect home in the perfect neighborhood, close to everything, and the kids loved it. But add job relocation to the mix and no matter how perfect the home is in every way; they can't take it with them to a new town. These clients are suddenly dissatisfied with their housing situation (they can't commute, after all) and their urgency to find a suitable place to live in that new town has set in.

Or let's take someone newly divorced. His or her dissatisfaction stems from the recent life change, not the home. Although he or she may have been perfectly happy with the current structure, the new single status demands a change of residence—whether it be to downsize, follow a dream, or forget the past. The urgency to move is now in play.

What about empty nesters? Again, their house didn't change; their lives did. They may no longer have a need for a large home with lots of bedrooms. Or maybe they want to pursue their dreams of retiring to the mountains, the ocean, or the city. As their children went off to college and began their own lives, the empty nesters' needs—and thus their relationship with their home—changed.

And sometimes people just fall out of love. It happens in relationships more often than most of us like to admit, and it happens with our homes even more frequently. It's that old case of "Well, it felt right at the time, so we did it!"

For many homebuyers, their current home may well have been just right for them at some point. But they're over it now… like a stale relationship with no spark. It could be the design or the dated décor, or the lack of energy efficiency. It might just be boredom and the desire to find someplace new. Either way, dissatisfaction has set in and a growing sense of urgency is finding its way into these homebuyers' hearts.

In all of these cases, dissatisfaction is the motivating factor when it comes to why people move.

JEREMIAH GORE
Mastery Level Insights

I typically spend a lot of time researching before buying a car, comparing all the information I can find about the targeted vehicle and its competitors. My most recent car purchase was different. One day I visited a friend who works in the car business, intending to take him out to lunch. While waiting for him, I wandered around the showroom and discovered a beautiful car that was a significant upgrade from my current ride and had far superior technology. Sitting in that car for a brief moment, I realized that my current car was no longer good enough for me. I immediately became dissatisfied, and I found myself unable to imagine driving my car home.

A dissatisfied buyer is motivated by a trigger event, and that event causes them to become a prospective shopper. The trigger event in my case was seeing an amazing car and then recognizing my own dissatisfaction. That's what motivated me to make the purchase. Similarly, many people who visit model homes don't realize how much they dislike their current homes until they see what's possible for their future.

Dissatisfaction Over Time

After thinking about different reasons people have for becoming dissatisfied, you may have realized that this isn't a kind of static emotion that goes nowhere. In fact, you may have noticed from your own personal experiences that dissatisfaction tends to grow over time. It's dynamic; once it starts, it can easily take on a life of its own.

As a rule, your home doesn't change as dramatically as your life. Over the last five years, has your home or your neighborhood changed all that much? Not really. But what about your life—does your life change over five years? You bet. Notice how our lives change *apart* from our homes. I call this the "dissatisfaction gap." The dissatisfaction gap grows over time as your life moves you away from your home.

The Dissatisfaction Gap

The dissatisfaction gap is real, but many homebuyers either don't realize it or don't want to share it. Many homebuyers don't want salespeople to know just how much dissatisfaction they feel and how urgent their need really is. Think about it. Have you ever heard a homebuyer say, "Oh, well we just started looking" or "We're not in a rush; we want to make sure we find the perfect place"? These statements are usually made in an attempt to convince the seller they won't be buying soon. Nope, no desperation, no sense of urgency there—everything's *juuuust* fine.

Maybe...maybe not.

Suppose a couple comes to your open house and tells you they've been in the market for four weeks. As a curious sales professional, you ask them why they're thinking about moving and they reply, "Oh, well our house is too small."

Now, what just happened...

No, wait. Think about what did *not* happen...

There's absolutely no way one of those people rolled out of bed that morning, walked into the kitchen, took a look around, and stated, "Say—this kitchen is too small! Now, how did that happen?" The fact is, that kitchen has been "too small" for a long time. And that means that person has been in the market for years!

> "When the 'why' is known, the sales process is so much easier and personalized to the customer."
> —Jaymie Dimbath, Vice President of Sales and Marketing

Application Break

- Think about the last three prospects you've worked with, whether they purchased from you or not. What likely drove them crazy in the home they lived in (or are still living in)? Frame that answer in emotional terms.

- For example, does your understanding stop at "Their current home is too small"? Or can you say, "They've got three growing children who are constantly bickering over sharing bedrooms. The tension in that house seems to be thick."

Let's go back to the very strong pre-COVID market of 2019…

How dissatisfied did homeowners have to be with their homes before they broke down and put it on the market? If you were there, you'd know it didn't take much: "Oh, look, honey, the counter tile is chipped. Let's sell. What did the neighbor get for his house? We'll add $20,000." That was the norm for many sellers at that point. A low threshold for dissatisfaction created an unrealistic sense of urgency that had people selling their homes left and right in an attempt to find the next best thing.

But that's simply not the case in a tougher market. When the market softens, people end up living with their dissatisfaction for long periods—they learn to adjust to and accept the situation. It takes a serious amount of dissatisfaction to get homeowners to budge when the market is softer. They're learning to live with the problem—until they can't stand it anymore, that is.

That's when they show up in your office…as the most motivated traffic you'll ever see!

So, are you convinced yet?

You should be, because if you don't understand the depth of your clients' dissatisfaction, you're in for a rough ride. Understand that dissatisfaction and you'll be a hero; miss it and you'll be facing a difficult sale—or maybe no sale at all.

Study Questions

1. How do you probe for home dissatisfaction without being intrusive?

2. Is it only *unhappy* circumstances that bring about home dissatisfaction? How can a happy circumstance trigger home dissatisfaction?

3. How would you monitor a client's dissatisfaction over time? Could you actually graph it?

Chapter Four

The Power of "Why?"

> *"It is a miracle that curiosity survives formal education."*
> – Einstein

So, you're probably thinking all you have to do is pinpoint your clients' dissatisfaction and you'll be home free. Sounds easy, right? Well, there's just one little, itty-bitty, teensy problem.

Your clients don't come in wearing their dissatisfaction on their sleeves. I mean, it's not like they just walk into your office with big scowls on their faces, lips twisted in disgust, and start unloading their housing problems on you. No, they don't *want* you to know how dissatisfied they are because they don't want to come off as desperate, or needy.

Until they trust you, the dissatisfaction they feel is strictly personal, not something to be discussed with a real estate salesperson. As far as you're concerned, they're happy to give you one of their standard lines such as "We're looking for a home in a good school district for the kids" or "We just want to downsize." Not to mention the dreaded, "Just looking."

You see, *trust* is the key that unlocks the door to understanding their dissatisfaction.

> "It's now more important than ever for a sales professional to understand why a customer is standing in front of them in their model home. If a sales professional can truly understand the buyer's 'why,' they can get on the buyer's mission and understand how to sell a home to them."
> —Scott Roulier, New Home Advisor

A salesperson in Florida shared with me a powerful example. She had met an older gentleman at an open house, and they had this conversation:

Salesperson: *"What has you in the market for a home?"*

Client: *"I'm downsizing."*

Salesperson: *"Tell me more about that. Why the need to downsize at this point?"*

Client: *"Well, it's just me. And, well, I dunno—I feel like I'm kicking around in my own house. It just doesn't work for me anymore."*

Salesperson: *"I don't want to be nosy—I just want to understand. Did something change in your life?"*

At this point, the gentleman looked very uncomfortable, even pained. He paused and then said, *"Well, my wife passed. Six months ago. And now, every time I turn a corner in that house, it's painful. I thought I was going to stay there forever, but I'm just miserable."*

Let me ask you a question, sales professional. How much do you think this guy wanted to share that story when he first walked through the door? Not much, right? But how much did he absolutely *need* someone to talk to, someone who understood, someone who cared? I would say a great deal.

This leads me to one of the most overlooked and underdeveloped traits of a successful salesperson in home sales. Well, in all sales really. It's ***the trait of deep curiosity.***

> **Curiosity is one of the most underdeveloped but incredibly powerful skill sets for sales professionals. And like any skill, it can be developed with focus and practice. Nurture a profound sense of curiosity and the sales will roll out in front of you!**

Have you ever known an insanely curious salesperson? I bet you have. In fact, you may have one of them on your team right now. You know that man or woman who just has to know exactly what makes his or her clients tick. He probes his clients tirelessly but respectfully for information and knows exactly the right questions to ask. She excels at building trust and her clients feel comfortable opening up. There's no shame in their game, and they won't rest until they fully understand the depth of their clients' dissatisfaction.

Alas, most salespeople are asking all the wrong questions from the start.

MARY BETH BERRY
Mastery Level Insights

Every customer has a story—a unique set of circumstances and life events that has brought them to your door. There is power in understanding our customer's "why," and it's our job to uncover that "why power" that will help motivate the customer to make a positive change.

> A truly great sales professional enters every sales interaction with the mindset: "I serve my customer best when I know them best." And they let that mindset drive them to an insane curiosity to uncover their customer's story.
>
> The number one way to do this? Be confident in your curiosity! Your openness and willingness to learn about your customer will provide them with the safe place they need to share their "why." You demonstrate through your open-ended questions, your welcoming body language, and your intense desire to listen. In such ways you can demonstrate that you genuinely care and that you can be trusted to help guide your customers through the homebuying process.
>
> It all starts by understanding "why" they began searching in the first place.

To get to the depth of any client's dissatisfaction, you have to take a whole new perspective on the discovery process. Most salespeople focus on the superficial, the surface problems: "Oh, you say your house is too big/too small" or "So, you're looking for a good school district." These surface problems are simply effects of the larger issues at hand, the root of the clients' dissatisfaction.

By focusing on the surface problems, you only get half the story. At this point, making a sale is a crapshoot. When getting to know prospective clients, focus on the root of their dissatisfaction above all else.

So, how do you do this? First off, don't be like most salespeople who are stuck on these "what" questions:

- *"What size home are you looking for?"*

- "What's your time frame?"
- "What's your price range?"
- "What's important to you in your new home?"

These aren't *bad* questions; they certainly have a time and place. But a salesperson can ask all of these questions and still not understand the root of the clients' dissatisfaction.

During a break in a training session, a brand-new salesperson asked me, "In your opinion, what's the most important question to ask in all of home sales?"

He was probably guessing I'd say any number of closing questions such as:

- "Would you like to buy this home?"
- "Would you like to make it yours?"
- "What's it going to take to get you to make a decision today?"

Did I respond with any of those? No, none of the above. In fact, I didn't even have to pause or hesitate with my answer. Do you know what the single most important question I ask all of my clients is, the question that gets to the root of their dissatisfaction?

> **The single most important question in homes sales is: "Why are you thinking it's time to move?"**

One. Simple. Question. That's all it takes. It's all about the "why." Make that your mantra: "It's all about the why." If you don't know the "why," then the "what" really doesn't matter.

> **Application Break**
>
> - What is the most natural way for you to ask the one simple motivation question—the "Why are you thinking about moving?" question? The only way to confirm what's natural to you is by practicing—out loud! I cannot stress this enough. You can't improve your performance by reading a book or attending a training session; it requires practicing *out loud*.
>
> - Try it now. Put this book down and test how you would ask the question. What is the most natural delivery? What are the right word choices and inflections? Practice this question until it's second nature to you.

Study Questions

1. How will you build trust with your homebuyers so they're willing to share personal stories with you?

2. What is the first question you can ask to determine a client's reason for dissatisfaction?

3. What is the difference between saying "Do you want to buy a new house?" and saying, "Tell me more about why you want to buy a new house"? How will your client respond to each of these?

Chapter Five

The Why Behind the "Why?"

The "Why?" question is critical. I repeat—the most important question in all of sales.

But we can't stop there because the real issues are rarely found at the surface level. Think again about that one person in your office who always seems to "get" the clients. If he were to stop with one question, he'd probably only get a partial answer. Instead, he keeps probing until he finds out the *real* reason, the emotional trigger that's causing their dissatisfaction.

Until we understand the clients' dissatisfaction *from an emotional level*, our job is only half done.

Let's see this in a case study. A gentleman meets a salesperson who proceeds to ask, "Why are you thinking it might be time to move?"

The prospect replies, "Our home is too small."

Where might the conversation go now? If typical, we would see something like this.

Salesperson: *"Oh, how big is your home?"*

Client: *"Fifteen hundred square feet, three bedrooms."*

Salesperson: *"And what are you looking for?"*

Client: *"Probably at least twenty-two hundred square feet, four bedrooms."*

Salesperson: *"Great, I know just the right home."*

Do you see the significant problem there? What exactly is the "right home?" And can we really say we have this figured out? It's bordering on arrogance to suggest having the right home at this point.

> **Your key phrase: "Tell me more about that…"**

But let's see the conversation go into a different direction, using one of the most powerful questions in all of sales: **"Tell me more about that…"**

Salesperson: *"You said your home is too small. Tell me more about that."*

Client: *"Well, the home was great when it was just my wife and me, but now our three girls are ten, twelve, and fifteen—it's cramped."*

Did that just change everything? You bet it did. But is there another level still—a deeper level of motivation? Let's see where this goes.

Salesperson: *"What specifically isn't working? What's most frustrating about the situation?"*

Client: *"Well, the home is eighty years old, and somehow back in those days, the builders didn't think you needed more than one bathroom. With three girls, it's kind of a problem."*

Kind of a problem? *Ya think?!* This guy is living in a home with three teenage girls and one bathroom. What do you think his life is like every morning at seven o'clock before school? And where does this guy shower—the YMCA?

Take a minute to reflect on this example. Why do you think that guy is dissatisfied with his home? Sure, the initial "why" led to stating the home is too small, but that's not the real reason. Plenty of people live in small homes and are completely satisfied. Plenty of people have only one bathroom and it works for them. So, what is it really?

MICHELLE BENDIEN
Mastery Level Insights

Every buyer has a story. Sometimes that story is happy, and sometimes the story is sad—but every homebuyer has a story. It's our job as sales professionals to give our customers a safe space and place to tell their story.

Does every homebuyer want to share their story? I believe so, but it may take a bit of time. They may not be willing to share their story with just anyone. They may want to make certain that we care enough to know their story first. Thus, the importance of coffee worthiness if you want to create the safe place that customers need if they're going to open up.

Get curious with focus statements like, "Tell me more," "Share with me," or "Help me to understand," and then dive deeper into the emotion behind their responses. After all, the emotion is where the magic lies.

> Why is this so important? Because in the absence of a story, we tend to create our own (often uninformed) version of the buyer's story. And we could be wrong—way wrong. Not only will this diminish the customer's experience, but it could lead us to take them to the wrong home.

Looking closer at the situation, we can see that the deeper "why" centered around bathroom count, but again—that's not the real reason. A deep dive into the deepest "why" ultimately would lead to the probable dissension and discord they experience on a daily level: the kids fighting over who gets to use the bathroom first; his wife tired and irritated that she can't get 15 minutes to put on her makeup in the morning; and his feeling frustrated with the constant arguments.

This guy isn't buying a bigger house or a bathroom; he's buying peace in his household.

Here's another example, courtesy of a sales representative in Houston.

Salesperson: *"Why are you thinking about moving?"*

Client: *"We're looking to move into the Williamson School District."*

Salesperson: *"Tell me more about that. What is it about the school district you're in now that isn't working?"*

Client: *"I just don't think they have the children's best interests in mind."*

Salesperson: *"Thanks for sharing that with me. It's so hard to entrust your children to someone else and then not have the sense they're being taken care of. If you don't mind, what specifically caused you to say it's time to move away?"*

Client: (After an awkward pause) *"Well, my son is getting bullied almost every day. I've talked to the principal and the superintendent, and they just promise to look into it. My son is starting middle school this year, and there's no way I can keep him there."*

Question: Do you think this guy wants to walk up to a salesperson and say, "Can you help me? My son is getting bullied, and I'm afraid I'm failing as a parent." Probably not. You see, it takes a certain amount of trust for clients to reveal the root of their dissatisfaction because sometimes the reasons can be painful or even humiliating. But that trust is established through a caring curiosity.

Until you can plumb the depths of your client's "why," you'll be forever stuck trying to sell with incomplete info. You'll leave them to figure it out on their own.

In these case studies, we've seen a similarity of focus; all have relied on deeper curiosity and the phrase, "Tell me more about that." In fact, we see a progression with each deeper question. We move from Level 1 to Level 3:

- **Level 1:** Broad Fact

- **Level 2:** Narrow Detail

- **Level 3:** Emotional Result

> *"A customer's 'why' is a culmination of things that led them to our door. They're not conscious of it and likely haven't pulled it all together, so getting curious and asking questions about what's going on in their lives now and tying things to what's not working allows us to build their memory and bring things to light in a more significant manner. The goal is for every guest to leave grateful they've found a solution to their 'why.'"*
> — Jen Collinsworth, Senior Vice President of Sales

It's important to understand that the highest form of selling is to meet clients in their emotional place—that is, in Level 3. When I understand the person's dissatisfaction on an emotional level, I can also provide an emotion-based solution.

Application Break

- Start practicing the "Tell me more about that" technique in your everyday life. Make it a point to use it tonight at dinner with your kids or when talking on the phone to a friend or when your spouse is downloading on the day. Then move on to the food server who waits on you, the receptionist at the dentist office who starts talking, or the taxi driver taking you to your appointment.

- "Tell me more about that" isn't only a great sales skill; it's a great life skill!

This is a long way from Sales 101; this is advanced. Think of the power of selling at this level! This chart gives you an idea of how the progression might work:

Level	Client	Salesperson
Level: Broad Fact (*"Why are you thinking about moving?"*)	"Our home is too small."	"Great. I can show you a larger home!"
Level 2: Narrow Detail (*"Tell me more about that…"*)	"We have three teenage girls plus my wife and I, all sharing one bathroom."	"Great. I can show you a home with more bathrooms."
Level 3: Emotional Result (*"May I ask how you're doing with that?"*)	"We're miserable. My girls fight every single morning. They just don't like each other."	"So, you're not just buying bathrooms; you're buying peace in your own home."

Can you see the progression? The deeper the knowledge of the client's dissatisfaction, especially at an emotional level, the easier it is to provide a positive emotional picture.

AMY O'CONNOR
Mastery Level Insights

Far too many salespeople rush through the discovery process with the buyer so they can get right down to selling. Here's the problem: You can't sell effectively if you don't know anything about the person in front of you. The most important sales question to ask is: *"Why are we talking?"*

You need to find a more eloquent and relational way to ask this question, but stay with the core principle. The single most important piece of information you can know about your prospect is their motivation for purchasing.

> The discovery process done well makes the buyer feel heard, appreciated, respected, and understood. Salespeople with mastery level discovery skills can learn more about their buyers in five minutes than their competition will ever know. And isn't that what all buyers want—to be heard and understood?
>
> If you can get your customer talking about the "why" of their situation, the rest of the sales presentation will roll out in front of you.

Study Questions

1. Problem solvers use the "Three Whys Down" questioning method (ask "Why?" three times in three different ways) to get beyond a surface issue to the true root cause of a problem. Practice doing this with a homebuyer situation.

2. When you find out the underlying reason for homebuyer dissatisfaction, what will you do with the information?

3. Think of a time when a client seemed ready to buy a house, but you just couldn't get him or her to move off the fence. What do you think the barriers were? What could you have done differently?

Chapter Six

Boldness in Questioning

At this point I need to stop and address an objection that I hear from time to time. It sounds something like this:

"People don't want to answer all these questions. I don't want to be intrusive and ruin the relationship."

Let's explore that just a bit.

If I asked you how much money you made last year you'd probably bristle and decline to answer. But when your accountant asks, it's not a big deal. If I asked you to talk about a personal physical problem, you might get offended. But you're very open about the issue when talking to your physician.

My point is that you must not confuse social norms with business realities. The probing questions that you ask of a customer are asked so that you can best serve their needs! You can't solve a problem that you don't understand. As with a physician or an attorney or an accountant, asking questions is about serving your customer.

With that context in mind, digging deep is not only appropriate but absolutely expected. So long as there's the presence of trust you can expect that a customer is going to open up to you.

Keep in mind also that these deeper questions to your prospects are open-ended. Asking "Tell me more" type questions gives room for the customer to share what's important while allowing them the freedom to share as much or as little as they choose.

All this leads to definitive soul searching for the sales pro. It's time to sit down and ask two serious questions. Be honest with yourself in answering each of them:

- Do you have the guts to ask the deep questions?

- Are you prepared to exercise your curiosity and dig even deeper?

Remember, this isn't about you; it's about your clients. You can serve them best when you know them deeply. Is that your mission?

> *"Do you mind if I ask you some quick questions in order to point you in the right direction? When I ask this, I see people stop and want to talk."*
> —Graeme Robertson, Community Sales Manager

I'm prepared to show you how to move forward in a structured and conversational way. But we have to be honest. Thorough discovery is not always comfortable. If it were, everyone would be doing it.

You see, most people opt to take the easiest route to get to where they want to go. But, as you already know, the easiest route doesn't always deliver the best results. If you yield to your discomfort, you'll miss out on the opportunity to serve at the highest possible level.

Make a decision right now to get to know your clients more deeply and more quickly than ever before. I'll show you the technique, but you have to bring the intention. All the technique in the world is meaningless without applying it, and application follows resolve.

So, ask yourself this: How deeply do you want to serve your clients?

From there, commit to understanding their dissatisfaction and everything else will follow.

For a deeper dive into this topic, pick up a copy of *Be Bold and Win the Sale*, available at the Shore Store (shop.jeffshore.com). In that book, I teach you how boldness is about service, and how you can overcome the most common discomforts you face in the sales process.

RYAN TAFT
Mastery Level Insights

Preference Questions vs. Decision Questions

When sales people utilize The 4:2 Formula, their confidence goes through the roof. The reason for that confidence is because they get to see the sales path roll out in front of them. In other words, they know which home they'll show the buyer, which objections are likely to appear, how to walk them through a home based on the buyer's story and…how to close.

When I'm out shopping as a customer, or even when I'm watching video shops, I notice that most people don't close with bold questions. In fact, I'd argue that all too often they don't close at all. They use preference questions. Here are a few examples.

- *"Isn't this kitchen great?"*
- *"Could you see yourself living here?"*
- *"So, what do you think?"*

To draw a distinct contrast to preference questions, let's define the word "decision." The first part, "de," means "of" or "from." The second part, "cision," comes from "to cut."

Decision = To Cut Off From

Decision questions cut off from all the other options they have been considering. This relieves brain strain! For example:

- "Is this your new kitchen?"
- "Did we find your new home?"
- "Do you want to purchase this home?"

It just takes the boldness to be direct and concise, but I'd argue that that is exactly what the customer wants you to do, as Jeff said in his book, *Be Bold and Win The Sale*.

Study Questions

1. What have you learned about yourself in this first section?

2. What is your personal area of discomfort in talking with clients?

3. What actions will you take to develop your curiosity and questioning skills?

SECTION 2:

♦ ♦ ♦

The Formula for Change

By now you have an understanding of dissatisfaction as a motivator. You understand that not only does dissatisfaction provide us with the desire to change our situation, but it also serves as the single most powerful force in creating urgency.

Think for a moment about that ideal client. You know, the young couple who bounced from one apartment to the other only to finally become dissatisfied with paying rent for a small, cramped space with no backyard. Or the middle-aged couple suddenly turned empty nesters in need of a smaller, more flexible home for their work-at-home lifestyle. These client pairs are dissatisfied with their current situations and have a desire to make a change. It's up to you as a salesperson to pinpoint the root of your clients' dissatisfaction and turn it into a tool to help them find the right homes to fit their needs.

In this section, I'll show you how your clients reach a decision point, how to utilize a powerful formula to evaluate every existing prospect, and how to apply that formula to every future prospect you will ever meet.

You'll even see yourself in this process because we're all motivated by dissatisfaction every day of our lives.

In short, this formula leverages the four factors that drive the decision to buy a house. In these four areas—two action motivators and two action inhibitors—you'll see the factors that cause your clients to make one of the most important purchasing decisions of their lifetime.

Chapter Seven

Motivation Factor #1: Current Dissatisfaction

Section 1 laid out the basis behind why people move. In it, we took a look at a few of the reasons, but we can sum it all up in one word: dissatisfaction. Here, we'll look at this action accelerator from a deeper perspective as we understand the *emotion* behind the situation.

At some point, people say to themselves, "I don't like this apartment anymore" or "Man, with six kids, this house isn't big enough." Maybe they say, "I need to entertain because of my job; I need a nicer place." Or "This neighborhood has gone downhill; I don't feel my kids are safe anymore." It may be any number of things—the amenities, the changes in the clients' lives, children moving out, a job transfer, or an elderly parent moving in.

I call this condition Current Dissatisfaction, and it has absolutely nothing to do with what a client is moving *to*. Rather, the Current Dissatisfaction focuses on what the homebuyer is moving *from*.

Whatever the reason for moving, the clients sense that something in their lives isn't right, that their housing situation is no longer satisfying. By the time they arrive at your doorstep, you can be assured that every prospective client you meet is on a mission to improve the quality of his or her life. After all, if there's nothing wrong with their lives now—if everything is rainbows and unicorns—well, why make a move?

Remember from Section 1 that clients' Current Dissatisfaction is not typically found on the surface? We have to ask questions, listen, and try to understand the factors motivating our clients to buy a home. Determining this motivation requires deeper probing.

This concept represents a dividing line between *average* and *great* sales professionals. Most salespeople will, if only by accident, stumble on their prospect's Current Dissatisfaction. But the key to leveraging that Current Dissatisfaction is understanding it on an *emotional* level.

> **People don't buy because of their dissatisfaction; they buy because of their emotional response to their dissatisfaction.**

This is a critically important principle to grasp: People don't buy because of their dissatisfaction; they buy because of their emotional response to their dissatisfaction. A prospect might say, "My home is too small," but the real motivation will have to do with his or her frustration in living in a small home. That could be tied to any number of things: friction between kids; lack of privacy; annoyance during dinner preparation; even embarrassment in having people over. Notice that these real issues are all primarily emotional, not logical.

Author and business entrepreneur Nido Qubein offers a helpful insight: "People don't buy products. They buy the solutions that the products represent."

As an example, a 30-something couple walks in and, by all appearances, are doing well financially. They pull up in a late-model SUV wearing trendy clothes and waving around the latest gadgets. If you were just a spectator looking in on the situation, you might make some assumptions about their jobs, their social status, and their spending power. But making assumptions doesn't get you any closer to the heart of the issue; it only sets you up for failure.

After a few minutes of introductions and chitchat, you ask these questions:

- What are you looking to spend?

- Where do you want to live?

- What kind of amenities are you hoping to find?

> "People don't buy products. They buy the solutions that the products represent."
> - Nido Qubein

After the usual responses about the neighborhood, kitchen is too small, living area is tiny, and so on, the truth comes out: Their current kitchen has outdated countertops; they have cracked marble tile in the entryway; the carpet is *shag*. Somewhere in the middle of all this explanation, the wife blurts out, "I'm just too embarrassed to have company over, and we need to start entertaining. I would die if my coworkers or my husband's ever saw our house!"

And there it is—at the emotional level. It isn't the countertops or the tile or the carpet. Those can all be fixed with remodeling. It's the emotional *embarrassment*. It's the Current Dissatisfaction motivating this couple to buy a newer, more stylish house.

JEREMIAH GORE
Mastery Level Insights

When I got remarried, I knew I was taking on a Herculean task: blending two families into one. It was like trying to make a smoothie with cereal and orange juice, two ingredients that refuse to get along. And to make matters worse, both my wife's daughter and my own were teenagers—creatures who have developed an allergy to sharing anything, especially bathrooms. I could already hear the battle cries echoing in my head every morning. I mean, forget World War III, this was going to be Bathroom War I! As someone who hates conflict, I knew I had to find a solution before my house turned into a battlefield.

A poor sales process would focus solely on my desire to have an additional bathroom. A great salesperson would focus on my mission. And what was that mission? To prevent the clash of the teenage titans and restore peace in the kingdom of the porcelain gods.

Following are three case studies that show how the dissatisfaction on the surface doesn't reveal the emotional factors that truly drive a decision.

Case Study #1: A man comes into a sales office and, upon questioning, shares that his home backs up to a busy street.

The salesperson responds, "Tell me more about that" and the prospect replies, "The street is where the teenagers go cruising on the weekends. Then they pull over to talk, but their radios are blaring. I have no peace and I also have safety concerns." The initial response ("busy street") is far too vague to constitute an action driver. Only with deeper probing do we understand the real concerns—peace and safety.

Case Study #2: A woman tells a Realtor she wants to downsize. Many salespeople would take this in the direction of "What size home do you have?" and "What size home are you looking for?" A better Realtor says, "Tell me more about that." He discovers that the woman has been hanging on to her large home for too long, that she took a huge cut in pay to keep her job and can no longer handle the payments. Her real motivation is financial peace, not square footage.

Case Study #3: A man at an open house says, "I'm tired of renting." The salesperson asks why, and he responds that there's an ongoing feud with the neighbors over the volume of their stereo, that the landlord refuses to do anything about it, and that he recently had his tires slashed. "Tired of renting" is *not* a motivation to move, but fear certainly is.

Consider these examples of common statements of motivation and where the actual dissatisfaction might lie:

Discovery Level One	Discovery Level Two	Discovery Level Three
Current home backs to busy street.	Lots of traffic thus a safety concern. (How many salespeople would have assumed a noise problem?)	Third time a family cat has been lost to traffic—a highly emotional issue.
Relocating from out of state.	This relocation is optional; the family is on a discovery trip.	Husband is excited about the move; wife is heavily resistant.
Couple looking for more bedrooms.	Currently living in a three-bedroom place looking for five.	Couple is newly engaged, both with kids from previous marriages.

Application Break

- Brainstorm different ways to say, "Tell me more about that." Understanding Current Dissatisfaction is always about digging far below the surface. If you can become familiar with several different probing questions, your questioning will come off more natural and less threatening.

- Whenever you meet a prospective client this week, think about the Three Whys. Commit to digging down to this third level of understanding. When you do, you'll find that this is the level where the emotion resides.

One last thing to know about the client's Current Dissatisfaction: It doesn't happen overnight. It brews and festers until your clients can't take it anymore. Usually by that point, they've already made it into your office.

This is good news. We've heard the dreaded words, "We just started looking." Typically, our hearts sink at that statement. We feel frustrated knowing people have to go through a long process, and they are just at the start, right?

Except for one thing—it's not true. They did not, in fact, "just start looking." They've been looking for a long time, certainly as long as they've lived with significant dissatisfaction.

> *"One of my salespeople recently sold a home to a police officer who had been transferred to a new department. The officer's daily commute to work had become considerably longer, and she was looking for a new home closer to her workplace. In addition, her aging mother wasn't able to sleep in an upstairs bedroom when she came to visit, which made finding a suitable home even more challenging. The salesperson's ability to develop a strong relationship with the customer, coupled with her understanding of the officer's dissatisfaction with her current home's location and the challenges presented by her mother's visits, allowed her to provide a solution that met the officer's needs. By leveraging her expertise and understanding all of the buyer's motivation and specific dissatisfaction, the salesperson was able to present a home that worked for the buyer. The buyer stopped at our office first and then visited competitors. She came back because she knew that our salesperson was on a mission to help her."*
> —Brad Tiffan, Vice President of Sales

The couple who walked in and told you their home is too small is an example. It's not like they woke up this very morning, got out of bed, looked around, and suddenly proclaimed, "Say, this house is too small! When did that happen? Honey, I don't know what plans we had today, but we're going house hunting instead."

> **Current Dissatisfaction brews over a long period, and it's always increasing.**

No. That home has been too small for years! The dissatisfaction has been brewing a long time. Now they can't take it anymore, and they land in your office.

The truth is, they wanted to move yesterday. Now it's your turn to help connect them with the Future Promise waiting for them.

Study Questions

1. When was the last time you bought a new home? How long were you living with your own Current Dissatisfaction before you started looking for something else?

2. What is your Current Dissatisfaction in your present home? Create a list and consider how your own dissatisfaction escalates over time. Then think about how your emotion rises with your dissatisfaction.

3. What would you do if one client admits to a Current Dissatisfaction, but the spouse or partner doesn't?

4. With your current clients, fill out the table of Discovery Levels 1, 2, and 3. (If you can't quite do this exercise now, you'll gain insights in the coming chapters, then come back to complete it.)

Chapter Eight

Motivation Factor #2: Future Promise

> *"As for the future, your task is not to foresee it, but to enable it."*
> – Antoine de Saint-Exupéry

If a compelling Current Dissatisfaction exists, there must also be an ideal and compelling Future Promise; that is the second of our motivation factors. The Future Promise represents the hopes and dreams of a new home and of a new life. It also represents the solution to the emotional pain of the Current Dissatisfaction.

Your client's Future Promise represents the picture in their minds of what their lives could be like. It's the hope of things to come when they move forward. It could be tied to the home itself, to the yard, to the neighborhood, to the schools, or to just about anything else the clients look forward to. Typically, it's a combination of all those things.

> **The Future Promise represents the hopes and dreams of the new home and of a new life.**

Specifically, the Future Promise is a loosely formed mental construct that guides clients on their search, a fuzzy image of an undefined ideal. You've likely heard prospects say something like, "I'll know it when I see it." Here's what I believe they're actually saying: *They'll know it when they see it!* The Future Promise is not always clear in the clients' minds, especially in the early part of the homebuying journey.

Let me ask you this: What do you suspect is behind all the design shows on HGTV? Or why are there racks of magazines with photos of beautiful kitchens? Is it to sell product? Of course, it is. But what's the appeal of these products? To have better countertops that last longer? Maybe. To have more efficient water usage with shiny new faucets? That has to be considered. But honestly, these products *play on the hopes and dreams of what could be*. They appeal to the motivation of Future Promise.

Like the Current Dissatisfaction, the Future Promise isn't fully understood until we uncover it on its *emotional* terms. It isn't only about the nice kitchen or another bedroom. It's about the pleasure of life. It's about the sense of peace when the kids have their own space. Or the vast yard space to be able to entertain that they're lacking today. Or the great room that allows for the ultimate in informal entertaining. Or the main bedroom suite that provides an escape from four active (and loud) children.

> **The Future Promise is all about the vision of a better life.**

Typically, too many salespeople get stuck on "What are you looking for?" After all, most have been trained that way. It's ingrained in their minds to look for the sale by meeting the obvious need. But this question should get at a more important point: "*Why* are you looking for it?" This is the deeper, emotional motivation that needs to be met.

Let's look at a few scenarios to discover the power of the Future Promise at a deeper level.

Scenario 1

Salesperson: *"How many bedrooms are you looking for?"*

Client: *"Four."*

Salesperson: *"OK, got it. And are you looking for a one-story or two-story?"*

WRONG! This follow-up question doesn't connect at the emotional level. Let's try that again.

Scenario 2

Salesperson: *"What are some of the 'must-haves' on your list?"*

Client: *"We need to have four bedrooms."*

Salesperson: *"OK, got it. Tell me more about that. Why four?"*

Client: *"We have two teenagers, a boy and a girl. Because of my job, sometimes I have to make overseas calls at odd hours. Right now, I work from a home office in the corner of the master bedroom. When I have to make these calls in the early hours, it's a real problem."*

As you can see in the second scenario, this buyer isn't simply buying another bedroom. He's buying both the pride of his own office space and a remedy to the inconvenience of early morning phone calls while his wife sleeps. In effect, he's buying a solution to his Current Dissatisfaction.

MARY BETH BERRY

Mastery Level Insights

"But what if the customer wants a bunch of *'must-haves'* that I *don't have*?" This is a common question asked by salespeople. I have two bits of good news:

Good news #1: There's no such thing as a "perfect" home. And if the perfect home DID exist, it certainly would not be for sale at a perfect price. We aren't looking for the perfect fit; we're looking for the *best* fit. Everyone compromises. Everyone. Find the best, not the perfect.

Good news #2: Customers don't buy products; they buy solutions to their problems.

Let me explain. I live in an area of the country where, due to the type of soil, basements are not very common. People move to this area from other parts of the country, and they list a basement as one of their "must-haves." Rather than saying, "I'm sorry. We don't sell basement homes here," I urge sales professionals to dig much deeper. Ask WHY they need a basement. Is it for added storage? A hobby room? Something else? What are they trying to store? How do they store it now? You get the picture.

If you understand the concern on a deep level it opens up creative solutions. Once again, the phrase "Tell me more…" will serve you well.

If you understand your customer well enough, you can sell their Future PROMISE rather than just a Future Product.

The top performing salesperson is wise to always consider the "why" behind the "what." Remember, every "what?" question demands a "why?" follow-up. For example:

Salesperson: *"What is most important to you in your new home?"*

Client: *"Yard space. We'd love to have at least eight thousand square feet."*

Salesperson: *"Tell me why eight thousand. How did you arrive at that?"*

Client: *"We're avid swimmers and would like to put in a large pool. But we also have two dogs so we need some lawn space."*

In this example, you learned important information to help you determine which home might be right to show them, and you also learned about their lives. This allows for a deeper sense of connection.

> **Application Break**
>
> If you're working with clients who have a hard time verbalizing what they're looking for ("We'll know it when we see it"), try to find the Future Promise by understanding more about the home they're in now. A good question to ask would be, *"Tell me about the home you're in right now. What do you love about, and what do you hate about it?"*

How Customers Make Decisions

The Future Promise provides the buyer with a mental framework for what their life will look like in their new home. This is an imaginative process that occurs largely in the subconscious. The customer is asking the question, "When I think about my future in this new home, how do I feel"?

We all make decisions according to the expected outcome. The role of the sales professional is to help the customer to imagine a life well-lived in their new home and to provide future emotional moments. This does not have to be sappy or syrupy, but it does need to provide a clear future reality in order to trigger such emotion.

Placing the furniture is an example of Future Promise. Asking about rear yard usage counts, as does inquiring about hobbies and interests.

The Current Dissatisfaction – Future Promise Connection

Before moving on to the next factor in our formula, here's one more intriguing thing to understand about Future Promise: A strong Future Promise can actually serve to boost the client's Current Dissatisfaction!

Let's suppose your best friend buys a brand-new car and wants to take you out to lunch to celebrate. Of course, she'll drive. You meet up somewhere and get out of your perfectly satisfactory car and into her new car. As you get in, you notice several cool things:

- That wonderful new car smell

- The push-button ignition that works while the key stays in her purse

- The back-up camera on the dashboard

- The air-conditioned seats

After lunch, your friend drops you off and you get back into your old car. Now what happens?

- You take a big whiff and ask, "What is that smell?"

- You have to fumble for your keys in your purse.

- You have to crank your head to look behind you when backing up.

- Your seat is blistering hot on this summer day.

Before you first sat in your friend's brand-new car, you were perfectly happy with your own. Where are you now? Pointed in the direction of a car dealership!

This works in home sales as well. Clients might be moderately dissatisfied with their current house but not enough to make a move. Not yet, anyway. They claim they're "just looking," and to a point, they actually believe that. Imagine, however, that they walk into a home with a tricked-out main suite. Or a house with lots of storage space, a high ceiling, large windows, a sitting room, a dual-sided fireplace. Or closets big enough to waltz in, a soaking tub with Jacuzzi jets, towel warmers…the dream bedroom.

> *"I can't sell a $500k countertop or flooring. I can sell a $500k solution to our prospect's mission. Without finding out the 'why,' we're just selling sticks and bricks."*
> —John Upchurch

Until now, they were fairly satisfied with their main bedroom suite. It got the job done and didn't cause any problems. Their Current Dissatisfaction was relatively low. But now they see an amazing Future Promise, and their Current Dissatisfaction skyrockets. Suddenly, their present bedroom seems tiny, plain, and boring compared to the tricked-out suite they saw in the house they were just shown. Now they're thinking about the inadequacies of their current home and how much better life could be in a new place with more features and better amenities.

> **A compelling Future Promise can elevate your client's Current Dissatisfaction.**

If your clients don't lead off by showing high Current Dissatisfaction, don't panic. It may be they haven't yet acknowledged the need at an emotional level because they don't know what's available. Sometimes Current Dissatisfaction develops once your clients see what options and amenities are available as part of the Future Promise.

Study Questions

1. Throughout your career, you've seen a lot of homes with wonderful amenities. If you were in the market for a new home now, what would you include in your Future Promise? Make a written list.

2. Compare your Future Promise list to the Current Dissatisfaction list you made for the last chapter. What

items might you add to your Current Dissatisfaction list given that you've thought about Future Promise?

3. Think about your current clients. How are they articulating their Current Dissatisfaction and Future Promise? How can you help them discuss and even write down their thoughts?

Chapter Nine

Inhibitor Factor #1: Cost

While the Current Dissatisfaction and the Future Promise work together to move clients forward, two inhibitors can hold them back. The first of these is cost. Let's define that; it's not as simple as it might seem.

Most homebuyers associate cost with the total price tag on a home, the bottom-line sales price as stated on the purchase agreement. We all know, of course, that one can't consider price alone. Cost is better defined as representing every "price" the client will have to pay, even the non-financial ones.

Here are examples of cost, both monetary and non-monetary:

- **Selling Price** – Think of the price as a value gauge on the home. The selling price is not in and of itself a financial burden unless the client is paying cash. But the price does represent a sense of comparative worth as well as being an indicator of the ability to qualify for a loan.

- **Payment** – The price is but a value gauge; the payment is where the rubber meets the road. The mortgage payment is the part that hurts every single month. The buyer asks, "What types of sacrifices will I have to make when I purchase this home? Can I still live the lifestyle I desire?

Will I have to suffer in terms of quality of vacations or how often we eat out?"

- **Time** – Buying a home and moving takes time. Your client has to take time from work or use weekends to find a home, get qualified, pack, unpack, and so on. Purchasing a home is not a simple endeavor; the process eats up a significant amount of time for any homebuyer.

- **Moving** – Imagine if I asked you to take two days off, and on day one instructed you to pack up your garage and let the boxes sit where they were. Then on day two, you'd unpack the boxes and put everything back. How would you feel about that? Horrified, probably! But your client has to think in terms of the whole house: all of the garage, all of the kitchen, all of the knickknacks collected over the years, all of the yard toys—ugh! Buying a home is a gigantic hassle and inconvenience is a huge cost.

- **Down payment** – Paying 20% down on a $500,000 home is $100,000. I don't know how else to look at it except saying that's a lot of money. Does your client really want to part with an amount that likely took years to acquire? Will the return be worthwhile? What are the other investment options for that cash? Will it drain their reserves?

- **New Costs** – Is there a homeowners' association with monthly fees? Will the taxes be higher in the new home versus the old home? Will the clients have to put their kids in a new school or even a private school? Will the energy bills cost more? Is there garbage service and will it have an out-of-pocket cost? And then there's always this thought: "What else am I missing?"

- **Compromise** – Every dollar spent is a dollar that's unavailable for something else. So, when clients buy a home, they're committing to that mortgage payment, often at the expense of other things they'd like to have and do (e.g., cars, vacations, private school, etc.).

> **The salesperson who thinks that cost only equals sales price is in for a difficult awakening!**

> **Application Break**
> Think of a client you recently sold a home to. What were the most significant aspects of cost, apart from the price? Now brainstorm the questions (in your own words) that might help you understand your client's cost concerns.

How Deals Destroy Value Perceptions

Undoubtedly, cost is a significant inhibitor. In fact, the cost factor scares a great many *salespeople.* That's one reason why many sales professionals take a proactive—though faulty—approach by talking about discounts and deals right off the bat. (Big mistake, by the way.)

Sellers who lead with their discount or their willingness to deal do more than just lower their profit. They cause a devaluing of the product. And not just a financial devaluing, either. Clients literally think less about what they're actually buying.

Consider the Macy's department store approach. When is Macy's *not* having a sale? And on top of the sale, how about its "Preferred Customer Coupon"? And the mysterious 50%-off rack in the corner, the one with the rider that says, "Today only—take an additional 25% off"?

At Macy's, while customers feel good about the discounted price, they also discount the quality of the merchandise. In their own minds, they think items that are easily obtained are lightly esteemed. "Yes, I got a good deal, but I'm not all that in love with the merchandise." Are you with me on this point?

Do this mental exercise. Do you have an item of clothing right now that you've owned for 30 days or more and still have the price tags attached? If you're like most people, the answer is "yes." Next question: Did you get it on sale? Again, the majority would say they did. Now think of an item of apparel—perhaps something you're wearing right now—that you paid full price for. How soon after you purchased it did you wear it? Right away, I bet.

> *"Through 2021 and 2022, the overall costs of materials and labor to build a new home increased to a level that started making families take a hard look at whether or not to move forward with a purchase decision. To further compound the costing effect, land development and dirt prices continued to rise. In an environment where builders were sometimes taking price increases multiple times a week, it became more important than ever for a sales consultant to identify and understand a buyer's needs so they could make an educated decision on a purchase quickly."*
> —Jordan Brown

Similarly, when a salesperson brings up discounts and encourages offers right off the bat, this devalues the perception of the home in the homebuyers' eyes. If this strategy is being encouraged, then the clients will question if the house was overpriced to begin with, and whether this discount strategy was already accounted for. So then, they suspect, the house isn't worth what's being asked. The perceived value has already dropped and may serve to steer them away from making an offer.

As a salesperson, you may actually be doing your clients a huge disservice by talking about discounts. You may, in all reality, be steering them *away* from the house of their dreams—their Future Promise!

MICHELLE BENDIEN
Mastery Level Insights

"Yay! I'm so excited! I get to pack up twenty years of stuff that I've accumulated over the years and move it across town! This is going to be so much fun!" (said no one—ever). The cost of moving goes far beyond price and payment. Just the hassle factor alone is real and painful, and it's an inhibitor that causes potential homebuyers to pump the brakes and ask themselves, "Is this really worth it?"

The key is to understand the pain before you get to any cost issue. Too often customers will bring up their concerns (price, payment, hassle, whatever) only to find that the salesperson offers some kind of discount or incentive. That's the wrong play. When you do that, you've taken every bullet out of the urgency gun. It's like going to a birthday party and within the first few minutes you open all the presents and eat all the cake. You're then left with, "Now what? Is that all you've got?"

Save your "gifts" until the end, after your customer finds the right home—the home that solves their dissatisfaction and has a great Future Promise! They'll have more value and meaning if you do. THEN you can address the cost issues.

As Jeff says, there's no better urgency than personal urgency—the urgency that brought them in to see you in the first place. Find that out first; then handle everything else.

Study Questions

1. How does a discounted price on a home make potential clients feel about the value of that home?

2. We've articulated some of the costs of buying a new home. What are some of the existing and potentially increasing costs of staying in their current home? How would you use this information to help clients who are struggling with the perceived cost of the new home based on its listed price?

3. If the cost of "hassle" weighs heavily with a client, what can you do to help overcome that hurdle?

4. "Time is money." How does working through a systematic process to getting homebuyers off the fence and into a new home quickly save them money?

Chapter Ten

Inhibitor Factor #2: Fear

The final factor is related to cost but is best approached from the emotional perspective. Though sometimes overlooked, the clients' level of fear is so important that it cannot be ignored. Even clients with a high Current Dissatisfaction and who have seen an incredible Future Promise can have an overwhelming and even debilitating level of fear.

Years ago, a resale client called me and said he desperately needed to sell his home and get it closed—*in the next 72 hours*. He was going through a messy divorce, and he needed this asset off the books in a hurry. That meant an all-cash deal at a deep discount. While the home's condition was a little rough, it had an amazing location and an incredible price.

I wasn't in a position to buy it at the time, but I figured I could get a fellow Realtor to bite. First, however, I offered it to my in-laws. I called the folks and rushed them over to show the home. I was so excited I couldn't stand it—a rare deal that comes along once in a blue moon.

My mother-in-law walked through the home and got an immediate negative impression: old carpet infested with cat fleas. My father-in-law noted the dry rot around the tub in the bathroom. I watched them view the home with disgust on their faces. I couldn't believe it; this was a rare opportunity, and they were consumed with cosmetic issues!

In the end, they passed on the home. I sold it all cash later that afternoon to a Realtor. An interesting side note: The home sold four years later for four times what the Realtor paid, a 400% value increase.

> **Even clients with a high Current Dissatisfaction and who have seen an incredible Future Promise can experience an overwhelming and even debilitating level of fear.**

To this day, my in-laws regret their short-sightedness. For the longest time, I thought they were simply foolish. But over time, I came to understand that their response wasn't unlike most people making a highly emotional decision. The fear is absolutely gripping.

The Sales *"Counselor"*

An important function of a real estate salesperson is to understand the homebuyers' fear, cope with it, and help them overcome it. This is where the term "sales counselor" comes into play. Whether you like it or not, you play the role of junior psychologist from time to time.

Yet too many salespeople are afraid to plumb the depths of their clients' fears. They worry that if clients talk about fear, it will elevate the concern and possibly spoil the sale. I disagree, and I advocate taking an entirely different approach.

As a salesperson, if I don't know what's bothering my clients, it doesn't lessen their fears. In fact, it may serve to *promote* those fears. They can feel they're all alone in this endeavor, that they're being misunderstood or even misinformed. This will heighten their emotions and especially their fear. And that's not good. This type of misunderstanding leads clients to distrust salespeople and believe all salespeople are just out to make that quick sale and disappear.

It pays to know what your clients' deepest fears are.

> "My sales consultant was having difficulty in getting a buyer to make a confident buying decision. When she analyzed the buyer's backstory, she discovered a ton of Current Dissatisfaction from the wife and none from the husband. The couple had recently retired, and the wife felt their current large, old home was sucking away precious time and money in maintenance. Her husband was not properly included in the discovery process.
>
> The sales consultant called the couple and asked to chat with the husband. She apologized for understanding his wife's resentment toward the house but not understanding why he was there. He said that he loves his wife, but he built the house with his brother who'd died a few years back. He just couldn't part with the house because of his brother. The sales consultant asked him if he thought his brother would rather have the home they built together continue to be a burden of time and money on him and his wife, or instead, understand the house had SERVED ITS PURPOSE and maybe it was time to let go and focus on what would make his life better and in the end, happier. That weekend the couple came back and signed an agreement."
>
> — Patrick Crocetta, Vice President Sales & Marketing

MICHELLE BENDIEN
Mastery Level Insights

Fear can be paralyzing and can stop your buyers from accomplishing their mission to improve their lives. We must help!

But what happens when *we* fear the fear, or just as bad—when we *ignore it*?

The answer: Nothing happens. Absolutely nothing. We become the sales-stopping moment because we didn't take the time (or the care) to get curious. We didn't allow our customers the opportunity to express their fears, to talk them out, and to understand what their level of fear was and where it was coming from. Perhaps if we had, we would be celebrating the closing of their beautiful new home versus commiserating over another missed opportunity.

This is where you need to channel the *counselor* part of your job. Lean in and listen with an empathetic ear. Let them express their concerns and you'll find you have an upper hand over every other salesperson.

Put yourself in their shoes for a moment if you will. A homebuyer's extensive fears can lead to a number of troubling questions:

- Do I really want to move in the first place? Am I *really* that unhappy with it? (Is my Current Dissatisfaction high enough?)

- Is this the right home? Will this meet my needs? (Do I see enough Future Promise?)

Inhibitor Factor #2: Fear

- Is this the right time to move, or should I wait?
- What will happen in the economy? In my job?
- What will my kids think? My neighbors? My parents?
- Are interest rates likely to go lower if I wait? Higher?
- What if I buy and then the price goes down?
- Are these the right schools?
- How long will the commute be?
- How much money will I have to spend after I move in?
- Will I regret this move?

Those fears, and many more, are real and ever-present. As a salesperson, you need to address them or, at the very least, acknowledge them. If fears aren't handled properly, they can be the cause for buyers' remorse. I believe the key to handling these fears is openness and honesty. Get your clients to talk through their fears and encourage them to hold nothing back.

> **Application Break**
>
> If you truly want to understand your client's fears, then provide an atmosphere of safety in which they feel free to share. Be open and honest with your intentions, explaining that you have their best interests in mind. *"I can help you so much more if I know what's holding you back. Tell me what concerns you about any part of this process."*

The Downside of Fear

In 2001, I seriously considered purchasing stock in Apple Computer, Inc. Like all other tech stocks, it had been hammered in the dot-com bust. But I was intrigued by this new device I had purchased: an iPod. Yes, I still have a first-generation iPod. It weighs about 5 pounds and holds maybe 50 songs, but it is a collector's item for sure!

Anyway, I didn't buy the stock. Why? Fear. I was reading the reports about the death of the tech sector, as if all things technological were gone from the planet forever (sounds dumb even to write that today). I listened to fearful media reports and couldn't pull the trigger. How do you suppose that decision worked out for me?

Make no mistake—undealt-with fear will cripple the decision-making process for any buyer. This is where top professionals come alongside and earn their commissions!

Inhibitor Factor #2: Fear

AMY O'CONNOR
Mastery Level Insights

A well-designed "Why you are smart to buy now" message builds buyer confidence in a couple of highly effective ways.

First, this type of message supports what the buyer already wants to believe. They already want to buy your product or service and are often seeking validation for their desire. So, give it to them! And make them feel good about buying!

Second, this approach provides the buyer with sound bites to share with others about the "why" behind their buying decision. Think about it: One of the reasons buyers hesitate is fear of judgment by their peers. By providing customers with simple, repeatable bullet points for why they should buy now, you create the confidence for them to handle any potential naysayers!

A confident customer is a decisive customer.

Study Questions

1. Do you have your own "Apple stock" story of an instance when you were fearful of taking action and today recognize that your "do nothing" action was a poor decision? How can you develop that into a personal story to share with your clients?

2. President Franklin Delano Roosevelt once said, "The only thing we have to fear is fear itself." He was speaking of the nameless, unreasoning, unjustified terror that puts us in a state of paralysis when we need to be moving

forward. How does talking with your clients about their homebuying fears help put their fears into a better perspective so they can be addressed and managed?

3. The list of fears that your clients might name (see above) includes several you can address with data and projections. How would you find this information, keep it current, and use it in a fact-based, unbiased format you can share with clients as you discuss these issues?

Chapter Eleven

The Buying Formula™

So far, we've discovered the four factors that influence a home-buying decision. They are:

- Motivation Factor #1: Current Dissatisfaction

- Motivation Factor #2: Future Promise

- Inhibitor Factor #1: Cost

- Inhibitor Factor #2: Fear

Now let's see how these factors work together.

Over a decade ago, I developed a formula I have since taught to thousands of sales professionals around the world. The formula has been proven over and over again, not only in my own experience, but in the experience of the sales professionals who've used it. You'll see it in every transaction you've ever had, and you can apply it to every future sale.

People buy when…

Current Dissatisfaction x Future Promise > Cost + Fear

I'll explain this in more detail, but for now, look closely and see how the formula works in your own experience. Recall someone who purchased from you recently. Or think of someone you've been working with who hasn't yet closed the deal. How do the categories apply?

> **If the clients' motivators don't carry more clout than their inhibitors, nothing happens.**

Let me break this down for you.

Like any math problem, all of the factors are variables. They can all be weighted or given varying importance. This formula takes everything into account, motivators and inhibitors alike. In effect, it puts them on a scale. But here's the bottom line of this formula: If the clients' *motivators* don't carry more clout than their *inhibitors*, nothing happens.

Let's suppose prospective homebuyers come to you with the following scenario:

A client bought a home at the height of the market. However, they bought in a less-desirable area because that's all they could afford at the time. Since then, the neighborhood has been in decline, and they're concerned with the safety of their children.

They've done some preliminary home search and have decided they want to purchase a home across town. To top it off, they've found one they love—a great location in the right school district with all the amenities they want.

However, the price exceeds what they want to spend. Not only that, but they've lost substantial equity in their current home in a market downturn and by leaving now would have to take a huge loss. They work in the high-tech industry, and they're concerned about the broad economy and the security of their jobs.

As a salesperson, here are some questions to ask yourself about this situation:

- How high is their Current Dissatisfaction? Pretty high, right?

- How high is their Future Promise? Also, very high.

- Their Cost (as defined earlier in the chapter)? WAY up there.

- How about their Fear? Sounds substantial.

For this client, *all* the factors are high. If they're to purchase, the variables need to be adjusted so the motivators outweigh the inhibitors.

As a salesperson, here are my options:

- Raise the Current Dissatisfaction

- Raise the Future Promise

- Lower the Cost

- Lower the Fear

> **Buyers often stagnate when paralyzed by their own fears. Something needs to change.**

So, let me ask you, what would you do? Think about it. Right now, the clients are stagnant and not moving forward, somewhat paralyzed by their fears. This means the scale is either equally balanced among all the factors or weighted toward the inhibitors. Something needs to change.

Hold that thought for a bit, and we'll get back to it. First, let's take a close look at the Buying Formula.

Observations on the Buying Formula

There are some things you need to know about the formula to fully get your hands around this powerful tool. Remember, people buy when:

Current Dissatisfaction x Future Promise > Cost + Fear

1. The formula is sequential; it's meant to be understood from left to right. Too many salespeople start with the cost side of the formula, which is a devastating mistake. If you want to have the best chance of getting them to make a decision, learn and highlight the Current Dissatisfaction first.

2. The left side of the formula is a multiplication function. What happens if either variable is a zero? We have a name for that kind of prospect: non-buyer. If the Current Dissatisfaction is a zero, nothing else matters—the formula will be forever out of balance.

3. A tie goes to the inhibitor. The only way to get your client to take action is to make certain the formula favors the left side.

The Buying Formula™

4. If both the Current Dissatisfaction and the Future Promise are enormous, how much work is needed on the Cost + Fear? Answer: very, very little. That's why we start with the left-side variables.

5. The variables in the formula change over time, sometimes for the good and sometimes for the bad. At the time the client purchases, the formula is weighted in the right direction. When remorse sets in and a homebuyer cancels, it's because the Cost + Fear weighting grew.

Now go back to the case study of the home purchased at the top of a hot market. Based on the principles you just learned, how would you go about solving the problem?

To start, you'd highlight the Current Dissatisfaction. In this case, the Current Dissatisfaction likely lies with the children's safety. Based on this assumption, two questions come to my mind. First, "Do you see the situation getting better or worse over time?" Second, "Are you concerned about the safety of your children if the neighborhood continues to deteriorate?"

The idea here is to point them in the direction of inevitability. They *have* to move; it's only a matter of timing. The longer they wait, the worse it will get and could one day involve a tragic incident. Or they may lose even more money due to their declining house value.

With the Current Dissatisfaction at a high level, it's time to cement the Future Promise. Your job is to confirm that the home has everything the clients are looking for—in location, in amenities, and in Future Promise. We can cement that with an instruction or comment like this:

"Prices rise and fall together across all markets. If you wait for the price of your home to go up, the price on the home you're looking for will also rise. It's best to base your decision on living in the right home and in the right neighborhood."

Or,

"The price of your home has fallen, but that's a short-term consideration. You don't want to cloud your long-term decisions with short-term factors. In the long term, what will be the wiser decision: staying there or moving here?" (I already know the answer to that since the Current Dissatisfaction is maxed out!)

Only when we've determined that the Current Dissatisfaction and Future Promise are both at a high level can we work on the Cost + Fear side of the formula. Had we started with Cost + Fear, we certainly would have had our hands full.

> "We discuss Current Dissatisfaction and Future Promise with every lead. It helps the sales team listen for trigger events when speaking with customers."
> —Tanner Jordan, Regional Sales Manager

> **Application Break**
>
> - Recall the last home you purchased. *Why* did you move? Was it out of Current Dissatisfaction? Future Promise? Did these outweigh Fear + Cost? Answer the question according to the formula and see if you can't find a direct application.
>
> - Now think about the last three homes you've sold. How did the formula apply to those three clients? Go through and fill in the blanks for each one. Remember the formula:
>
>   ***Current Dissatisfaction x Future Promise > Cost + Fear***
>
> - Most important, think of three clients you're working with today. Where are they stuck? Are they stuck in Fear? Why haven't they purchased yet? Is it because of Cost? The answer is in the formula, and when you adjust the variables, you'll free up the person for further actions.

Jeff Shore: A Personal Case Study

Let me share a little about the last time I moved so that you can see how the formula applies.

My wife and I had been in our home for 14 years. We moved in when our son, our oldest, was starting high school. The younger of his two sisters was in the fourth grade at the time. By the time they all left for college we were living in a home that was too large for just two people, we had five acres that needed to be maintained, we had a pool that we didn't use, and there was no reason to be near the school our children had attended.

That was our Current Dissatisfaction; let's look at the Future Promise.

We were looking for something that matched our changed lifestyle. That meant something closer to the center of town with significantly less land but still a lot of privacy. We wanted a home in a wooded setting that had all we need for our lifestyle: home office, drop-dead gorgeous kitchen, painting room for my wife, space for guests, bonus room for the ping-pong table, and a setup that was dog friendly.

We did have Cost concerns since we were moving to a more expensive area and would be paying more for the home. Our taxes would also increase; as might our utility bills. Our current home had been completely remodeled, so we might have to invest in the new place to meet our design tastes.

Finally, we had Fear. Was this the right time to make this move? What was happening in the market? Could we sell our home for enough? Should we sell first and then purchase? Should we hold onto our current home and risk carrying two payments? What if a flood of foreclosures hit the market—would that affect home values?

Later in this book I'll circle back to these four factors I mentioned. For now, let's look at our actual shopping journey.

It really started *years* ago. As soon as our oldest went away to college, our home got larger and grew larger still as each child moved out. It's safe to say we had been thinking about this for years, but our dissatisfaction factor five years previous was too low to initiate action. On a 1-to-10 dissatisfaction scale, we were probably at a 2.

When our youngest graduated from college and promptly moved to Seattle to take a job with Amazon, our dissatisfaction escalated. We started modestly snooping around. Like most buyers, that meant spending time online and getting a sense of what's out there. I would suggest, however, that our Current Dissatisfaction at the time was no higher than a 5—not enough to make a move.

Then something interesting happened. We started to look at homes and see the Future Promise they held. We discovered an amazing phenomenon, something I mentioned in Chapter Eight: when our Future Promise went up, our Current Dissatisfaction went up with it. We saw what could be, and it escalated our desire to move from where we were. Our Current Dissatisfaction rose to the 7-to-8 level.

Alas, the Cost + Fear was still high, especially since we hadn't seen a lot of activity on our current home. Do we take the risk of buying without selling?

We got to the point where the formula balanced out:

Current Dissatisfaction x Future Promise = Cost + Fear

Question: Given that formula, would we sell the home and move? NO! The CD multiplied by the FP must be *greater than* the C+F. In order to move, the motivators must *exceed* the inhibitors.

It wasn't until we found the perfect home that we decided to move. And when we found that home, something interesting happened. Our sky-high Future Promise pulled our Current Dissatisfaction UP!

I don't know about you, but this tool excites me! Understanding and applying the formula gives me a new way to look at my clients. I gain insight as to how they think, how they make decisions, and what the roadblocks to buying might be. I can then move them out of Fear + Cost and into Current Dissatisfaction x Future Promise. How cool is that?

Putting the Formula to Work

> **Understanding and applying the formula gives me a new way to look at my clients. I gain insights as to how they think, how they make decisions, and what their roadblocks to buying might be.**

Even with this tremendous tool at your disposal, there's one more piece of the sales puzzle to consider—the structure or the "how to"—and that's where we're going next.

Coming up, I'll show you a sales structure that complements the formula. It's simple, intuitive, conversational, and in no way manipulative. One of the surest ways to kill any future sales is to have clients walk away feeling tricked. This destroys trust, and in our profession, trust is paramount. After all, we're dealing with peoples' homes, the place where they need to feel absolutely secure and satisfied.

As promised in an earlier chapter, when you know your clients well enough, they'll literally show you how to sell them a home. The sales path will lay itself out right in front of you. Your job will then be to guide them down that path.

Ready to get started?

RYAN TAFT
Mastery Level Insights

It's one thing to uncover the CD, FP and the CF... it's another to remember it. Two questions might come to mind. First is *why* do you need to remember the Buying Formula and second is *how* do you remember it?

There are a few reasons to take note of your customer's motivators and inhibitors. You can:

- *Personalize your follow-up*
- *Be prepared for the return appointment*
- *Manage the backlog (each backlog call revisits the formula)*
- *Address buyer's remorse with the buyer's mission and emotion*

So how do you keep track of the elements of the formula? The obvious answer is to put your notes into your CRM.

I can already hear the groans of, "But Ryan, I don't have any time to add notes into the system." First, I disagree. I believe we have time for things we value. But I am not going to leave you hanging with that, as I do have a great solution here: Leverage the tech.

After each interaction with a buyer, open up your voice memo app on your phone and record what you learned. You can add this into your CRM during some downtime. Some systems even allow you to import the audio recording! I placed a voice memo icon on my Apple watch so I can talk directly into my watch without having to get my phone to do it!

If it's important, you'll give it your attention. And make no mistake about it. When it comes to knowing your customers and recalling the details of their lives—that's important!

Study Questions

1. If you know your prospects have zero Current Dissatisfaction, how likely are they to really be in the market for a home?

2. How does the buying formula help explain the conflicting thoughts homebuyers struggle with as they work through the decision process?

3. Where have you focused your efforts in the past (which of the four factors)? Where do you expect to focus in the future?

4. What will you do when your clients are stuck in the situation of the left side of the formula equaling the right side?

5. How does the buying formula apply to the last time you moved?

SECTION 3:

♦ ♦ ♦

The Sales 4:2 Formula

Now, you have a good understanding of the factors that motivate your clients to make important purchasing decisions like buying a home. People purchase when:

Current Dissatisfaction x Future Promise > Cost + Fear

So, the next big question is, how do we get the information we need about these four factors? How do we determine the varying levels of the different factors in the formula? And how do we do it with every single client?

As I mentioned before, your client won't just waltz into your office and lay down his or her hopes and fears just like that. No, that would be too easy. Besides, part of your job as a salesperson is to use your detective skills to sniff out deeper emotional reasons behind their impetus to buy.

So, do I just hand you a set of questions with instructions to memorize them verbatim?

Well, not exactly. Let's take a look at what works.

Chapter Twelve

Scripting the Presentation

> **Scripts are great...when they're *your* scripts!**

Think back to the first sales you ever made. Chances are, you used at least parts of a standardized script you'd learned in training. And although the script probably wasn't that exciting by the time you practiced it for the 27th time, it worked. Ask veteran salespeople and they'll likely tell you the best way to learn to sell is by using a structured questioning pattern, like a script. And a script is essentially that, a structured questioning pattern.

Here's the problem: Too many salespeople get stuck as they struggle to remember the lines of the script. They stammer and strain to come up with the exact wording, especially in the stressful heat of the moment.

And, yet, learning a strategically structured sales pattern *is* vital to the success of any sales presentation. In fact, just learning it isn't enough. It must be drilled so deeply into the subconscious that you don't have to think about it. With the process deeply ingrained, you're freed to connect with your clients on an emotionally deep level. Once you have it down, there's no longer a need for the script. You know the pattern and can adapt it for your client. In fact, that structure must be so deeply ingrained into your mind that you don't even have to think about it—you've become unconsciously competent.

Here's an interesting paradox; it might sound strange, but let me put this out there. Sales professionals must master their presentations so well that they become liberated from thinking about their presentations.

Wait! Say that again?

> ***Sales professionals must master***
> ***their presentations so well***
> ***that they become liberated from thinking***
> ***about their presentations.***

OK, let's think this through.

My son Kevin was quite the actor all through school, culminating in playing every actor's dream role his senior year in college: Willy Loman in *Death of a Salesman*. One thing about Kevin—he always had his lines down well before he was required to. He memorized as quickly as he could. As soon as he got the script, he was committing every line to his subconscious.

I asked Kevin why he was dedicated to memorizing the lines so early. His response made perfect sense and provides great insight for salespeople. To make the transition, simply insert "selling" whenever you see "acting."

In Kevin's words:

> *"Acting is not simply the sharing of lines. It's all about the connection with the person in front of you. When I'm acting, it's critical that I not be thinking about my lines. To do so would cost me—I wouldn't be able to deeply connect with my partner. Great*

> *acting is when the lines are down so solidly that you don't have to think about the lines. Instead, you think about the nuances of the interaction with the person standing in front of you."*

As you can see, it's the same thing with a salesperson. Like an actor, you have to "learn your lines." If you fail to do a good job at learning them, you might get stuck just when the action gets going. But those who have learned the script inside and out can take liberties, do a little improvising, and still stay right on track with the script. You haven't sacrificed your structured sales pattern.

That's what it truly means to have your presentation down solid. It's so ingrained in your memory that you don't even have to think about it. Instead, you're free to think about what's most important.

Your client!

> **Sales professionals must master their presentations so well that they're liberated from thinking about the presentation; they're freed up to focus on the client!**

You become free to respond to what you learn, to probe deeper, to understand the emotion behind the statement. You go with the flow of your clients, making a connection and fully listening to what they have to say.

If only all salespeople handled their clients like this, right? Instead, too many get stuck thinking about their next lines or aiming to impart a bit of trivial wisdom on their clients. When they do this, they're not really paying attention to the deeper messages the clients need them to hear. This eventually drives clients away.

When I first read *The Seven Habits of Highly Successful People*, I came across this gem of an idea from the late Stephen Covey in discussing Habit Five: "Seek First to Understand, Then to Be Understood." Covey said, "Most people do not listen with the intent to understand; they listen with the intent to respond."

Ouch. I felt like I'd been kicked in the gut on that one. It cut me to the core.

Some of you know the feeling of halfway listening to a prospect and the whole time thinking, "When you shut up, I have something powerful to say." But when you do this, you're not *really* listening with the intent to deeply understand.

It's this kind of thinking that puts you in a position of not focusing on the client at all. Instead, you're more focused on yourself and whether you've got your presentation down.

However, when you have your presentation perfected, you're now free to not think about it at all. You have the freedom to understand your clients on dramatically deep levels.

But Whose Script???

I'm a big fan of scripting out the perfect presentation. I am NOT a fan of simply memorizing and reciting someone else's presentation. You need to deliver the perfect presentation… in your own voice.

Customers can smell a memorized script from a mile away. It's unnatural for everyone involved when we try to recite someone else's lines. I'm all about being my authentic self, and that simply doesn't happen when I'm forced to deliver someone else's version of the sales presentation.

Having said that, I wholeheartedly endorse the concept of perfecting the way that you deliver your sales messages. Write it down. Work on it with your manager. Practice it over and over again. But first make it your own.

JEREMIAH GORE
Mastery Level Insights

Imagine a potential homebuyer walking into your open house or sales office. You're a pro and you know what you're doing, but as soon as you start talking you realize that the client is somewhat disinterested and seems to be checking the phone rather than engaging in conversation.

You start to panic, but then you remember two things. One, that your customer is nervous about *all* salespeople, and that the behavior is normal. Two, that you're well-prepared, and you have practiced for this moment. Your commitment to well-delivered discovery will carry you through.

You press on with your discovery so you can learn the customer's story. With your persistent but polite curiosity, the customer eventually opens up about their current dissatisfactions, future promise, costs, and fears.

If you're a veteran, you've lived that exact scenario a thousand times.

Structuring your sales presentations will guide you through difficult situations and keep you on track, but don't rely on simply knowing the steps. A well-performed and personalized script will only work through practice—just make sure that practice isn't being done with that customer who just walked in the door!

> *"Our sales team has used the 4:2 Formula to turn their sales process into muscle memory. It lays out the path for giving the customer a best-in-class new home purchase experience."*
> —Cristi Green

The Key to Effective Skill Development

How does one reach this level of proficiency? Your initial response was probably to say, "Practice!" And you'd be partially right. There's no question; practice is critical to success in any endeavor. But it's not enough.

Too many sales professionals practice only as long as they're required to do so. They practice in a training session or, if they're ambitious, in the car from time to time. Top professionals know it takes more than just practicing once or twice. The best of the best practice until they're tired of the sound of their own voice…and they practice more.

In short, it's not just about practicing; it's about *repetition*. As the saying goes, "Amateurs practice until they get it right. Professionals practice until they can't get it wrong." Truer words were never spoken. Great performances—in music, in theater, in athletics, *and* in sales—are based on endless repetition.

> *"The destination called mastery lies on a road called repetition."*
> – Jeff Shore

> **Application Break**
>
> - Try this self-training exercise: Think of one technique, however small, that you might be able to perfect through repetition. Perhaps it's how you explain a contract clause or multi-generational housing options. Or maybe it's simply how you exchange names when someone first walks into your open house.
>
> - Practice that technique ten times out loud, working on the specific tone and phrasing. Then record on your smart phone and listen back. Adjust the presentation, practice out loud five more times, then record it again.
>
> - Practice sounds monotonous and, like playing the scales on the piano, it can be. But the repetition cements proper technique into your brain. Start with something small and really nail it. You'll see the effect it can have the next time you use that technique.

The chapters that follow lay out the opportunity to revolutionize the first several minutes of your sales presentation. Most important, you'll learn more critical information about your clients in the first five minutes than most people learn in the entire presentation.

> **Amateurs practice until they get it right. Professionals practice until they can't get it wrong.**

But the execution of the principles is up to you. Sure, I'll show you how to practice repeatedly, but it will only be through your personal fortitude that you can take your presentation from good to great.

Study Questions

1. When was the last time you actually practiced something, so you knew it cold? (That bit of Shakespeare you had to memorize in high school English?)

2. Have you read Stephen Covey's book, *The Seven Habits of Highly Effective People*? If not, at least give it a skim. How can you apply some of his suggestions to improve the effectiveness of your listening skills, especially from Habit Five?

3. How well do you really listen? If you're the kind of person who likes to prepare a response while "listening" or jump in before people finish their thoughts, how will you break these bad habits?

Chapter Thirteen

Why vs. What

> *Always the beautiful answer who asks a more beautiful question."*
> – E.E. Cummings

In the next chapter, I'll share with you The 4:2 Formula, the pattern that will provide the structure you need to understand your clients and, based on that understanding, how you can accomplish the elusive sales nirvana called "mutual purpose."

The 4:2 Formula relies heavily on "why" questions vs. "what" questions. This is important because "why" questions help your clients talk about the real motivations that have them looking for a home and the deeper reasons behind the "what" factors. Once you know those "why" reasons, it's fairly simple to figure out the "what" that will be the solution to their dilemma. Chapter 6 spoke in depth about the difference between "what" and "why"; however, let's get to an even deeper level than that.

> **You need to ask yourself: "Am I a *why* salesperson or a *what* salesperson?"**

Here's a problem that I see in training sessions all the time: salespeople who are unconsciously competent at the *wrong things*. The fact is the overwhelming percentage of salespeople are stuck on "what" questions. They ask these what questions almost automatically, firing them off at their clients like a shotgun:

- *"What are you looking for in a home?"*
- *"What's your price point?"*
- *"What's your time frame"?*

Even in training sessions, in situations when I explicitly instruct them to ask "why" instead of "what" questions, they can't help it—a "what" question comes out.

Such is the power of habits, which is exactly why we're talking about this. I know old habits die hard, but we need to have this conversation. You won't be able to master the 4:2 pattern by blending it with an archaic and outdated method. My challenge is to begin harnessing the power of "why" so you might see how your sales approach changes for the better.

What happens when you rely too much on "what" questions? Tell me if this sounds familiar.

> *"The buyer's 'why' is both the source of their motivation and the driver of their urgency. Too many new home sales reps miss this and focus more on what they have to sell than on helping the buyer accomplish what they want. Understanding the importance of the buyer's 'why' helps keep our sales team grounded in the idea that the sale is not about us; it's about the customer."*
> —Kelvey Benward, Division Sales Manager

Salesperson: *"What's your time frame"?*

Buyer: *"We're in no rush."*

Salesperson: *"What's your price point"?*

Buyer: *"We're flexible."*

Salesperson: *"What kind of home are you looking for"?*

Buyer: *"We'll know it when we see it."*

All of those responses are frustrating, but the customer was just answering the best way they knew how. "What" questions often serve only to shut down the conversation.

Application Break

- To practice your "why" questions, start with something very, very common like bedroom count. Most salespeople learn the bedroom count early on in the process; at times it's the first piece of information we receive about a new client. A minority of salespeople dig deeper to find the "why" behind the "what."

- Build this into your discovery habit. As soon as you ascertain the bedroom count (either because you asked or they offered), immediately ask the reasons behind the bedroom count. "OK—three bedrooms? Obviously a main bedroom for you. How will the other two be used?"

- You could find that the "why" response might lead you to understand that "three bedrooms" might not be necessary at all! (More about that later in the book.)

In the implementation section, I'll offer specific drills to break those old habits and replace them with new healthier sales behaviors.

For now, just be aware. When you catch yourself asking "what" questions, stop and think them through. Make a conscious effort to ask "why" questions with each and every client you work with. Have your coworkers, spouse, or a good friend listen to your presentation and point this out. A conscious effort to change your approach is the only way to affect long-term change.

Just be aware—that's only half the battle.

MARY BETH BERRY
Mastery Level Insights

"Check yourself before you wreck yourself." – A cute bumper sticker

How can you "check yourself" to see if you're actually asking "why" vs. "what" questions?

You can start by going back and reading your notes in your CRM. If your notes contain mostly facts—bedrooms, square footage, prequal information, time frame, etc.—you're most likely only asking "what" style questions.

However, if your notes are full of the buyers' stories—the names of family, trigger events, life events, issues, challenges, emotion words, etc.—there's a high likelihood you're asking "why" questions. (Bonus: Follow-up is WAY more fun when you have these types of notes!)

Don't "wreck yourself" by only asking "what." Find your buyer's "why"!

Study Questions

1. Why are "why" questions so powerful?

2. If you can, record yourself giving your sales presentation or role modeling a client interaction with a friend or family member. Listen to the recording and jot down the questions you asked. How many were "what" and how many were "why" questions?

3. How would you convert your most common "what" questions to "why" questions?

Chapter Fourteen

The 4:2 Formula® Progression

> **Sales conversations can be cooperative or combative. Which approach do you think your clients want to experience?**

The 4:2 Formula is all about getting to know the clients on a deep level and allowing the sale to roll out in front of you. It's a cooperative approach. You're using the information the client is giving to you to help them narrow their focus and find the right home.

This is not to suggest that, in using this technique, you'll find your demonstration skills to be unimportant (they are!) or that you don't have to close the sale (you do!); it's just not the focus of this book.

That said, if you get The 4:2 Formula right, you'll find that showing your client the right home is infinitely easier. You'll find the close is completely conversational and entirely logical to both parties. The 4:2 Formula is a tool that serves you throughout the sales process.

> The goal in the demonstration is *not* to get your clients excited about seeing a home. The goal is to get to know your clients so well that you are excited about showing them the right home.

OK, so let's have a look at the entire process from the top down:

The 4:2 Formula = 4 Discovery Categories + 2 Summary Questions

The 4 Discovery Categories:
- ✓ Relationship Building
- ✓ Motivation Questions
- ✓ Current Dissatisfaction Questions
- ✓ Future Promise Questions

The 2 Summary Questions:
- ✓ The Summary Dissatisfaction Question
- ✓ The Summary Solution Question

THE 4:2 FORMULA®						
4 Discovery Categories				2 Vision Agreements		
1. Relationship Question	2. Motivation Question	3. Dissatisfaction Question	4. Future Promise Question	1. Summary Dissatisfaction Question	2. Summary Solution Question	

As we continue, you'll understand that the purpose of the 4:2 Formula is to use the "4"—the initial categories of questions—to get to the "2"—the underlying cause and solution. You see, the "2" is where the money is. This is where you establish a shared mission and where you offer clients a viable solution. It's a beautiful thing.

When you have completed The 4:2 progression, you will have established mutual purpose, a shared vision regarding where you are and where you're going. You'll be on the same page with your clients and have proven you have their best interests in mind.

Too many clients see the sales presentation as an "us vs. them" endeavor. Alas, many salespeople see it the same way. They take a *Glengarry Glen Ross* manipulative mindset into the meeting with a new client. That is, they believe (or have been trained) that sales is about trickery and manipulation.

I'll assume that doesn't represent your wishes. Frankly, if it did, you would have bailed out on this book by now! I'm here to talk to those who see sales as a valuable service to their clients, and those who see salespeople as contributing to the societal good. I suggest we do this most effectively when we seek to join our clients in their quest to improve their own lives.

> **Too many clients see the sales presentation as an "us vs. them" endeavor. You need to prove otherwise.**

> *"The 4:2 Formula helps the sales team focus on the most important aspects of the sales process and provides them with a consistent framework for approaching each interaction with a customer. By being focused on the customer's needs and providing tailored solutions, this proven technique has led to increased confidence, better performance for the sales team and stronger customer relationships."*
> — Dolly Majumdar

Having a mutual purpose with your client catapults you to a different plane of operation within the sales process. Mutual purpose is about being on the same page with clients in helping them achieve their goals. It's also about agreeing with them on how their lives need to improve and how you can help. Having a mutual purpose makes the rest of the conversation silky smooth because you're now both working toward the same goal.

With mutual purpose, you'll move beyond salesperson and into the much-coveted role of Trusted Advisor.

So, are you ready to establish mutual purpose with your clients? Well then, let's do it!

RYAN TAFT
Mastery Level Insights

The key word in the phrase "Trusted Advisor" is "Trusted." I see many sales people violate that trust in the middle of their 4:2 Formula discovery. Here's what it typically sounds like:

> Salesperson: *"What has you thinking about making a move?"*
> Buyer: *"Well, my neighborhood is going downhill a bit."*
> Salesperson (with a cheesy smile): *"I totally get it. So, a new neighborhood that has a fresh look to it is important to you, wouldn't you agree?"*

I'll wait right here if you need to throw up.

Seriously, if you're looking to create mutual purpose, you can't turn into a cheeseball or try to sell in the middle of your 4:2 discovery. It kills all trust in an instant.

THERE IS NO SELLING AND NO SOLVING!

> Holding back your solutions is a discipline and will require practice. Stay focused on the goal of mutual purpose. Once that's achieved (after the 4:2 Formula discovery), buyers will seek out your solutions because they know you truly understand their mission.

Study Questions

1. Why is achieving a mutual purpose valuable?

2. Think back on your most recent half-dozen clients. How many of those interactions could be characterized as having mutual purpose?

3. Pick one or two of these that weren't successful. What do you know about the client that would have helped you become a Trusted Advisor?

Chapter Fifteen

Discovery Category #1: Relationship Building

> *"To be trusted is a greater compliment than being loved."*
> – George MacDonald

The first step in the sales structure is to establish a deep sense of trust as a foundation for the buyer-seller relationship. That might sound like I'm channeling Captain Obvious here, but I'm going to put some new spins on the idea.

Let's talk about what we're trying to do—and what we're *not* trying to do.

From time to time, I hear a salesperson (usually a long-time veteran) say something like this: "I don't care if they like me; I just want them to buy from me!"

Let me ask you this: Is it possible to sell a home to someone who doesn't like you? Yes, it's possible, *but it's really, really hard!*

> **People like to do business with people who are likable.**

117

Would you buy something from someone you didn't like? Surely you have, but you probably don't remember that person and if you do, that memory isn't positive.

Now think about a time you purchased something from someone you really liked. You probably remember that person fairly well; you might even still have his or her business card hanging on your fridge. You probably recall liking the person because he or she seemed genuinely interested in you and your best interests. Chances are you wouldn't hesitate to refer that person to your friends and family.

This gives us an understanding as to why likability is a critically important variable in the study of influence theory. In fact, it's one of the six principles highlighted by Robert Cialdini in his landmark book *Influence: The Psychology of Persuasion* (an absolute must-read for every salesperson).

> *"Few people would be surprised to learn that, as a rule, we most prefer to say yes to the requests of someone we know and like. What might be startling to note, however, is that this simple rule is used in hundreds of ways by total strangers to get us to comply with their requests."* (Cialdini)

Being likable has proven scientific benefits for a salesperson. But can the pursuit of likability go too far? Of course, it can. Sometimes too much of a good thing is, well, just too much. I've seen many a salesperson take this to a level that actually cripples the sales process. Maybe you've experienced this yourself. Or perhaps you've seen another salesperson in your office attempting the overly friendly approach, only to get burned in the end.

They try to become fast friends and proceed to lose their objectivity. They also worry about offending the clients, even becoming afraid to voice their opinion or object to something that's not in their clients' best interest.

Remember, it's your responsibility as a Trusted Advisor to educate your clients about the best solutions for them. You're not there primarily to make a new friend—although it's great when it does happen. You're there to make a sale. Don't forget that!

Let me offer you this mindset; it's a concept with which I've gotten a lot of traction with salespeople.

The goal is not to develop your new BFF (remember, you're a Trusted Advisor). Nor is it to find someone to vacation with (you have plenty of those). In fact, those things involve too much pressure, too much commitment from both parties. Therefore, the goal of your relationship needs to be simpler than that.

Stop for a moment and ask yourself this question:

"Am I coffee worthy? Five minutes into this conversation would this prospect want to have a cup of coffee with me?"

Consider the question from your own perspective. What are characteristics of a person *you* would want to have a cup of coffee with? Go ahead, list them on paper. What kinds of qualities do you come up with?

- Friendly

- Interested in me

- Engaged and engaging

- Good listener

- Good-natured

- Expressive body language

- Excellent eye contact

- Confident

Aren't those the very attributes you would look for when you meet someone for the first time?

Now, imagine you were meeting a salesperson who shared exactly those qualities. Would you be OK with the thought of having coffee with him or her?

> **Make it your goal to be deemed "coffee worthy" within the first three minutes of the conversation.**

The coffee worthy test gives us a different standard for the rapport-building process. It's about purpose and intentionality more than about technique and scripts. In fact, I'm purposely omitting ideas on how to chitchat with your client because being coffee worthy isn't something you can pull off based on a script. Let's face it; if you're incapable of starting a conversation with a prospect, I can't help you!

But if your mindset is right, if you approach the conversation with intentionality, if you're committed to being as coffee worthy as you know how to be—you'll be there!

I recommend starting off your client meeting with at least 30 seconds in coffee worthy conversation. It can be longer than that, but I encourage you to let your clients decide. Remember, the purpose of this time is to build a foundation of trust that will lead to asking my first discovery questions.

> **Application Break**
>
> Make a list of the characteristics that would make you "coffee worthy." Then apply that list to your opening conversations. What, specifically, can you do to promote this opinion with your new prospect?

MARY BETH BERRY
Mastery Level Insights

You only get one shot at a first impression. Cliché but true.

And let's face it, because of pre-conceived notions and stereotypes, salespeople have an uphill battle when it comes to winning over our customers.

For his book *To Sell Is Human*, Daniel Pink surveyed thousands of people to see what words they associated with salespeople. The number one word? "Pushy." Yuck! That is NOT you! But it is important to understand that, as a profession, we have a reputation to repair before we can move forward with helping people to accomplish their goals.

Don't underestimate the power of being coffee worthy right out of the gate. We want to prove to our buyers that we care about them as human beings and that we can be trusted to help them on this incredible buying journey. The relationship is where we demonstrate that we're on a mission to understand and serve our buyers—not on a mission for a commission.

Starting the Conversation

The opening conversation with new clients should be organic, flowing naturally in the moment. That said, when you meet someone for the first time at an open house or in a model home, it can feel anything but natural. So having a "go-to" opening question or conversation starter is essential. Have it "at the ready" for when the door suddenly swings open, and you need to get a conversation started in a hurry.

Here are several "starter" questions that might help you develop an instinctive "go-to" conversation opener. Note that they all serve as relationship foundation questions.

- Any question regarding the weather. (That's why God made weather—so that salespeople can start a conversation!)

- Any question that allows for personalization (a car, sweatshirt, bumper sticker—anything that promotes a connection).

- "How is your day going so far?"

- "So, you're out shopping for a home. How's that going for you?"

- "How goes the home shopping? Are you having fun?"

NOTE: The following are NOT relationship questions:

- "What brought you out today?"

- "How did you find us?"

- "Is this your first time here?"

- "Are you in the market for a home?"

These questions go *against* our principle of relationship building. They imply you're more interested in talking about the sale than in building the foundation for a trust relationship.

> **Application Break**
>
> Do you have a "go-to" rapport-building question? Try experimenting with different approaches to the greeting. It keeps you fresh and makes you sound more interesting. Overusing the same approach can make it all sound canned to the prospect.

Permission to Question

> Asking permission to question is inherently respectful and it sends a message that you're acting in your client's best interest right from the start.

So many salespeople struggle with what can be the awkward transition between building rapport and discovery. In fact, many get so into connecting with their client, they're at a loss as to how to bring the conversation back to business without losing the comfort and trust they'd just worked so hard to build.

I've got a solution for that. It's a technique called "Permission to Question," and it serves as an effective bridge between rapport building and discovery. By practicing this powerful tool with each of your clients in the rapport and discovery phase, you'll find it becomes second nature and your discussions will flow smoother and more productively.

AMY O'CONNOR
Mastery Level Insights

"Permission to question" is a short, simple technique that lets the buyer know what you're doing and why you're doing it when you start asking them questions.

"Permission to question" gives the buyer a sense of control. It's respectful, it lets them know this won't take very long, and it indicates that these questions are in their best interest. Once they've said yes, they're now committed, and the law of commitment kicks in. This means that they'll be inclined to give you deeper and more honest answers—it's a win-win!

Here's how it works. When you believe you have built the needed rapport, say to your client:

"Can I ask you a few quick questions so I can lead you in the right direction?"

Simple, yes? Indeed. Simple—and incredibly powerful!

Let's break it down. Let me share the key components of the "permission question."

- *"Can I..." (or "May I..." if you're a stickler for good grammar)*
  What are you trying to communicate here? Respect. One of a prospect's greatest fears is that a salesperson will take control of the conversation against their will. Asking

permission says to the prospect, "You call the shots." By doing this, you put people at ease, allowing them a safe opportunity to open up.

- *"...a few quick questions..."*
  You're trying to let clients know this process will be painless and won't take long. They can get very uncomfortable when they don't know where the conversation is headed. Further, many clients are highly conscientious of their time. This way, you're letting them know you value their time and won't be taking up their entire afternoon.

- *"...so that..."*
  You want to communicate that this is for the *client*, not for *you*. You can serve clients best when you know them best. This shows you're genuinely interested in them.

> *"Permission to Question is probably my favorite strategy because it sets the stage for the entire 4:2 Formula. So many people walk through our doors and may not know what to expect, and a lot of the time salespeople assume these prospects 'know the drill.' We need to assume they don't, and tell them what they can expect to talk through, and what the ultimate goal is. 'I'm going to ask you a few quick questions so I can point you in the direction of the best fit, whether that's here or in another one of our communities! Sound good?' (shortened version). This gives us the opportunity to set the stage but kick-starts the 'yes' pattern with the prospect."*
> —Kaylie Austin, Division Sales Manager

(For more on the power of this question, I recommend reading Cialdini's book *Influence: The Psychology of Persuasion*. Focus on the principles of commitment and consistency.)

When you ask for permission to ask questions, your clients will say "yes" the overwhelming majority of the time, assuming you have a rapport in place. That's a critically important assumption, and it explains why we start the 4:2 progression with rapport building. But if you do this right, you put those clients into a position of being willing to answer just about any question you ask them.

Considering that position, I suggest it would be a good time to ask them the most important question in sales—the motivation question.

Study Questions

1. Have you read Robert Cialdini's book *Influence: The Psychology of Persuasion?* If not, at least skim it or watch an overview on YouTube. What are your persuasion strengths and weaknesses?

2. Jot down five or six of the typical conversation starters you use with potential clients. Now look at them critically; are they relationship questions? If not, how could you improve them for better relationship building?

3. Why would YOU want to have coffee with YOU? How could you make yourself even more coffee worthy?

Chapter Sixteen

Discovery Category #2: Motivation Questions

> **The most important question in all of home sales: "Why are you thinking about moving?"**

By now, you probably realize there's nothing more important to learn about your clients than the reason why they're moving in the first place. Their motivation tells a great deal about so many areas of their life, especially when that question is coupled with "tell me more about that" and other follow-up questions.

Consider this exchange between a salesperson and a client:

> Salesperson: *"Tell me why you're wanting to move in the first place."*
>
> Client: *"Our home is too large, and we're thinking about downsizing."*
>
> Salesperson: *"Tell me more about that. What's changed?"*
>
> Client: *"Well, our kids are gone, and we have a three-thousand-square-foot home. It's just the two of us now

and we find ourselves doing a lot more traveling than before. We don't need a large home; we need more of a place to crash but something that's still big enough for grandkids down the road."

Salesperson: *"Got it. That makes sense. And why now? Has something changed recently to spur the decision to move"?*

Client: *"We were talking last night about our desire to be debt free. If we sell the big home and downsize, we can accomplish that goal."*

Consider that the salesperson didn't ask a single "what"-based question. Everything was "why"-based and open-ended. So, what did she discover about her buyer?

- Motivation for moving

- Approximate size of the home

- Bedroom count

- Price point

- Interests

- Family information

- Desire for financial freedom

Look at that list! That's more than most salespeople determine in 30 minutes! Oh, and one more thing—that entire dialogue took just 30 seconds!

As you've noticed, when you ask the right question and you lead with a "why," you'll discover the motivation early on; this will shorten the presentation dramatically. That means less frustration for you, more time saved on the clients' end, and you get to the close more quickly.

> **The key to asking the motivation question is to ask it conversationally and casually.**

The key to asking the motivation question effectively lies in asking it conversationally. That's right—it has to sound like a part of the conversation. If it sounds like an interrogation, you're sunk. Your clients will feel cornered, as if they're no longer in control. If it sounds like you're reading from a script, forget it.

You have to ask the question as if you had run into a friend from high school at the grocery school. And that means practice. Practice until it's so natural that it sounds like you're asking it for the very first time. Practice until it's so ingrained in you that you don't have to think about the question. At that point you're free to interact with the clients, noting the nuances of their responses and seeking to understand the deeper messages behind them.

Here are sample motivation questions to get you started in developing the phrasing that works best for you:

- *"So why are you thinking about moving?"*

- *"So, you're out shopping for a home. What got you thinking that it might be time to move?"*

- *"What was it that triggered your home search?"*
- *"What has you out shopping for a home?"*
- *"What has you in the market for a new home?"*

> **Application Break**
>
> Practice, practice, and practice some more this three-step process: 1) Relationship building; 2) Permission to Question; 3) Motivation Question. Get those down pat; they need to be absolutely seamless. Of course, it's best to practice with others before you begin to implement the technique with clients.

The final section of this book lays out a practice regimen strictly for this portion of the sales process. This practice regimen will walk you through the simple progression of:

- ✓ Relationship-building conversation
- ✓ Permission to question
- ✓ Motivation question with follow-ups ("Tell me more…")

Discovery Category #2: Motivation Questions

> *"'What is going on in your life that has you looking to make a move?' This is my favorite motivation question. It allows the customer to open up. You have no idea where the customer will take you when they begin to answer this question. I've had some jaw-dropping responses. As a result, the connection made with the customer as they answered this question opened the door to continue moving forward. We now get to join their journey, which will allow us the opportunity to learn their current dissatisfaction and future promise."*
> — Ross Norman, Sales Manager

I cannot emphasize enough the importance of getting this three-part opening down solid, buried deep into your unconscious competence. Remember, you're like an actor learning his lines; you must live and breathe your character, learning it inside and out. If you sound like you're scripted, if you sound like you're strained, if you stutter or stumble or in any way show a lack of confidence, you're hosed.

I don't know about you, but I'm excited! Here we are, not two minutes into the conversation and already we've established ourselves as coffee worthy while learning vitally important pieces of information about our client. Whoever said that sales had to be painful?

Make this an enjoyable process for both you and your customer, and you'll be well on your way to becoming a Trusted Advisor.

MICHELLE BENDIEN
Mastery Level Insights

A salesperson friend of mine named Andy shared a story of when he didn't get curious enough with his homebuyers and how it impacted their experience. It was an older couple that had stated they wanted to downsize—the maintenance was too much. "Got it!" (or so Andy thought).

Throughout the conversation, Andy couldn't help but notice that the wife was painfully quiet. Andy, being the jovial guy that he is, started cracking jokes and being silly—doing everything he could to get her out of her shell.

At one point the husband pulled him off to the side and apologized for his wife's demeanor. He explained, "She's having a hard time dealing with all of this." Andy then learned that the husband was diagnosed with terminal cancer. He knew his wife wouldn't be able to maintain the home they raised their kids in on her own, and it would be too difficult for her to sell or move after he passed.

Now you know the story. She loved her husband, she loved her home, and she was losing both. Double whammy. Andy had to think back on all the potentially insensitive things he'd said and done prior to knowing and understanding the buyer's "why."

Lesson painfully learned.

Study Questions

1. Closed questions that can be answered with yes or no tend to close off discussions. Open-ended questions like "why?" and requests like "tell me more" draw out deeper information. Make a list of five closed questions you have

used in the past and then convert them into "tell me more" and "why?" questions.

2. Test the closed and open questions you listed with friends or family members. What do you observe?

3. How does this approach to questioning improve things for you and for your clients?

Chapter Seventeen

Discovery Category #3: Current Dissatisfaction

> "Dissatisfaction with possession and achievement is one of the requisites to further achievement."
> – John Hope

You know about the so-called tire kickers out there—those people who will never purchase and just waste your time. This might come as a surprise, but I don't believe in any such thing. In fact, I believe that labeling a prospect as a "tire kicker" gives me a convenient excuse for why I didn't sell them a home.

Here's the deal: By virtue of the fact that people visited your website, or called you, or showed up in your office—trust me, they are legitimate prospects. How can I be sure of this fact? Because of an important principle: *There's no such thing as a perfect home.* Today, they're living in a flawed home. They've contacted your office to do something about it.

Understand this: Everyone compromises. Everyone. Even Bill Gates compromised on the last home he purchased. With the last home he bought, he had to compromise on the size of the lot.

Everyone has to compromise because the absolutely perfect home doesn't exist. In fact, you compromised when you first acquired the home you're in right now. Don't tell me there are people out there who have no dissatisfaction. It might be a low level of satisfaction, but there's always something.

It's that dissatisfaction that drives clients through our doors. If everything were perfect in the home they live in today, they wouldn't be here (as discussed in Sections 1 and 2, remember?).

Buying a home involves a certain degree of psychological compromise. The job of the sales professional is to determine the "acceptable level of dissatisfaction." That term defines the way that the homebuyer copes with his or her expectations. (Note: You probably don't want to use the phrase "acceptable level of dissatisfaction" in a sales presentation!)

If you'd like an illustration of this principle, watch one episode of House Hunters on HGTV. See if the narration doesn't start this way:

> *"Jack and Barbara have outgrown their two-bedroom apartment. It was perfect when it was just the two of them, but when their fourth child came along, they knew they had to move. Jack and Barbara are in the market for a seven-bedroom, eight thousand-square-foot home with a view of the ocean and twenty groomed acres, and their budget is $200,000."*

OK, so it's not that dramatic, but you get the picture. The key is to watch the *end* of the show and see what they bought. I guarantee you it's *nothing* like what they said they wanted! Chances are, Jack and Barbara found their "acceptable level of dissatisfaction" in a four-bedroom ranch with a finished basement and a modest backyard. No, they won't be grooming ponies on the property, but the home fits their needs and their budget, and their kids can even get a dog.

Why are they excited about something that fell so far short of their initial description? Because everyone compromises. Everyone.

> **Buying a home forces people to determine their acceptable level of dissatisfaction.**

Bear in mind that the longer people stay in their homes, the more that dissatisfaction rises (as discussed in Section 1). When the dissatisfaction they feel is high enough, they come through your door—that's just the way it works.

Your job as a Trusted Advisor is to identify those areas of dissatisfaction by asking your client open-ended questions about what's wrong right now. Too many salespeople gloss over this part of the process; they're too eager to whip up a list of properties and whisk the clients out of their office and into an open house. These salespeople are doing nothing more than spinning their wheels! There's no solution if there isn't first a problem identified!

Here's what you need to find out before you can even consider finding your prospects the right home:

- What's wrong with the home they're in now?

- Why can't they stay there?

- What would they have to change if they were going to stay?

- What causes them frustration and angst?

Here are some questions that might help you get there:

- "What is it that you really don't like about the home you're in now?"

- "What will you be happy to leave behind when you move?"

- "What causes you frustration in your current home?"

- "Is there anything about your home right now that embarrasses you when guests come over?"

- "If you had thirty thousand dollars to spend on fixing up the home you're in now, where would you spend it?"

> **Application Break**
>
> Determine your most powerful dissatisfaction question and incorporate it into your sales presentation immediately. Commit to following up with "Tell me more about that" every single time.

Now, keep in mind, there are two important things to know in our discussion on Current Dissatisfaction:

1) Sometimes the buyer's Motivation and Current Dissatisfaction are one and the same. For example, if you ask a couple why they're thinking about moving, they might just tell you that they hate their home, that they've outgrown the space, and that they can't move soon enough. That answer encompasses both Motivation and Current Dissatisfaction. If that's the case, be sure to pay attention to point #2.

Discovery Category #3: Current Dissatisfaction

> *"It's like landing an airplane; if you don't understand your buyer's current dissatisfaction then you have no runway. So, when you try and present a solution, you can't land the plane because you didn't understand your buyer's actual needs to begin with."*
> —Taylor Humphrey, Director of Sales & Marketing

2) It's about the why behind the "why." You can't fully understand the clients' Current Dissatisfaction until you understand it on an emotional level. People don't move because of their dissatisfaction; they move because of the *pain* associated with their dissatisfaction. I can't emphasize enough just how important it is to understand the emotional impact of your clients' Current Dissatisfaction.

When working with your clients it's imperative that you resist the temptation to move too quickly into what the clients want. By understanding the Current Dissatisfaction well enough, you'll also understand the Future Promise to a large extent.

JEREMIAH GORE
Mastery Level Insights

Stop me if you've heard this one.

You and the family are out to dinner, ready to have someone else cook for you for the night. Rather than ask you any questions about what you might like, the waiter immediately begins listing everything on the menu in excruciating detail. The guy is listing the actual ingredients in the nachos!

If you had a waiter do that, you might feel like you're being bombarded with information that is not only useless but distracting to your decision-making efforts. It would also seem that the waiter doesn't really care about your preferences or needs and is just going through the motions. Overall, it could make the dining experience less enjoyable and potentially lead you to leave without ordering anything.

Instead of trying to impress our customers with how much you know about your product offerings, first dive deep into their Current Dissatisfaction. While you may be eager to share your answers to their problem, make sure you fully understand their pain before prescribing the solution.

Try to be better than the average waiter!

Study Questions

1. What goes wrong when you start showing homes to clients before you understand their Current Dissatisfaction?

2. Why is it valuable to go deeper than mere dissatisfaction to truly understand the clients' pain?

3. Current Dissatisfaction generally increases over time. How can you discuss this with clients to help them be ready to act on their dissatisfaction sooner rather than later?

Chapter Eighteen

Discovery Category #4: Future Promise

> *"People don't buy products; they buy the solutions that the products represent."*
> – Nido Qubein

We've seen the first three steps of the sales process: Relationship, Motivation, and Current Dissatisfaction. Only when we have fully understood and internalized these steps can we effectively reach step four: Future Promise.

The Future Promise encompasses the solution to their problem. Remember how Nido Qubein put it ever so eloquently: "People don't buy products. They buy the solutions that the products represent."

The Future Promise that you've helped outline for your clients represents their dream and their vision. It's what awaits them on the other side of the process of buying a home. The Future Promise is the light at the end of the tunnel for your homebuyers.

Determining the Future Promise is critical because it opens you up to an amazing depth of knowledge about your clients' hopes and dreams. You have to understand, your prospects have been thinking about their Future Promise for months, maybe even years. Why do you think magazines like *Better Homes and Gardens* and shows like *House Hunters* exist? They fuel the Future Promise.

Homebuilders construct model homes and hire interior designers to deck them out in high fashion in order to show the prospective buyers what their Future Promise might look like. A home stager creates a dream home out of an ordinary A-frame. That's all about maximizing the Future Promise. In short, if your clients can't come up with a clear vision of the Future Promise—no sale.

As a sales professional, it's your responsibility—no, it's your *duty*—to not only identify the Future Promise, but also understand *why* the clients desire such things. Without this, you're doing yourself and your clients a huge disservice.

And here we are—back to the "why."

> "The future belongs to those who believe in the beauty of their dreams."
> – Eleanor Roosevelt

It's not enough that the clients want four bedrooms. How they live their lives is what really counts: a spare room for company, separate bedrooms for the kids, or a home office for Mom.

It's not enough that clients want a large yard. It's what that large yard represents: getting a dog for the kids, grilling out during the 4th of July, inviting the family over for their son's graduation. It's the freedom to enjoy time with their family and be able to have the things they want.

Even the location is a massively subjective variable. Some folks want nothing more than the peace and quiet of a country lifestyle while others may want a fast-paced environment with everything in walking distance. What might be a killer location to you may not be to me, and vice versa.

Often, the Future Promise becomes obvious by simply looking at the Current Dissatisfaction. But what about those clients for whom the Current Dissatisfaction is initially not that strong? Good news: A compelling Future Promise can actually *create* Current Dissatisfaction.

When buyers see how wonderful their lives can be, they also reflect on what they have now. It causes them to compare their current home (not good) to your beautiful home (big life improvement). Suddenly, the homebuyers realize they've been missing out.

I remember walking the exhibit floor at the International Builder Show and seeing an interesting display. A lighting company had set up a bed in their display area to demonstrate their product.

Here's how it worked. Suppose it's three in the morning and you have to get up to do what you do at three in the morning. Under the carpet next to the bed is a sensor that picks up the fact that you've stood up in the middle of the night in a dark bedroom. At this point, low-level lights go on to illuminate the baseboards from your bed to your bathroom.

Did you just have the same impression I had? I thought, "That's the coolest thing I've ever seen in my life." But what was the basis for my enthusiasm? Several years ago, I absolutely crushed my big toe on a doorjamb walking around in the middle of the night. I mean to tell you, I dropped onto the bathroom floor in agony. It's still a painful memory.

> **Sometimes a compelling Future Promise creates a Dissatisfaction in the prospect's mind.**

After that episode, I thought I'd solved the problem by installing a motion detector nightlight. It proved to be an adequate fix, except that it was glaringly bright and stayed on for too long, small annoyances compared to slamming my toe again. My Current Dissatisfaction had subsided—until I saw an amazing Future Promise. Suddenly I hated my nightlight, and my Current Dissatisfaction soared all over again.

> **Application Break**
>
> How would you phrase the perfect Future Promise question? Practice several different questions out loud and determine what sounds right for your style. Then work these questions into your presentation as soon as possible. (Don't forget the "Tell me more about that"!)

MICHELLE BENDIEN
Mastery Level Insights

A few years ago, my husband and I wanted to downsize. We sold quickly and found ourselves in a desperate situation to find a new home. We settled on a place that was a disaster on the inside, but the outside was great—a pond with a beautiful fountain and landscaping to shield us from the surrounding homes.

We bought it, and we immediately changed everything on the inside—and I do mean everything. It was a beautiful situation…until it wasn't.

> As it turned out, we hated the neighborhood. Don't get me wrong; the neighbors were lovely people, but they didn't have the same passion to keep up their homes the way we did. We found ourselves in a situation where we knew that this was not going to be our *forever* home, but we weren't actively looking either.
>
> Out of the blue, my husband informed me that he saw a home newly listed for sale. It was situated on a secluded wooded site, and it might be worth checking it out. We did, and that same evening I was writing a contract.
>
> In an instant, our Future Promise was so great that our current home became unbearable. We *had* to move. Future Promise raises Dissatisfaction and Dissatisfaction raises Future Promise.

Must-Haves vs. Would-Like-To-Haves

The Future Promise is about identifying your clients' ideal. Remember, they all have two lists in their heads:

1. The "Must-Haves"

2. The "Would-Like-To-Haves"

Don't be dissuaded by clients with Future Promises that are initially too high. Remember, there's no such thing as perfect. The clients will compromise—they have to. Everyone does.

Make sure, though, that you've delineated between what the clients must have and what they would like to have before moving to the next step. As I mentioned earlier, many salespeople want to move straight to the show-and-tell.

> *"I feel great knowing that my sales team is not just trying to sell a home, but selling a solution to help the prospect. We care, and it shows."*
> —John Upchurch

Here are some sample questions that will help you develop the perfect phrasing for your own Future Promise questions:

- *"What are some of the "must-haves on your list?" ("And what else?")*

- *"What are some of the things about your old home that you'd bring over to your new one if you could?"*

- *"What have you seen that you really like?"*

- *"Describe some of the elements of your dream home."*

- *"Are there certain areas of the home that are important to you? Describe your ideal area."*

- *"Describe what a great Saturday morning would look like in your new home."*

Study Questions

1. How will you help clients with unrealistic "must-haves" to compromise and still be delighted?

2. Just as we asked "why" to understand the pain of the Current Dissatisfaction, we ask "why" again to understand the deeper elements of the Future Promise. Why is it important to understand the passion that drives these needs?

3. How does helping the clients articulate a Future Promise make the whole homebuying process more effective and more enjoyable for both the clients and you?

Chapter Nineteen

The Vision Agreements

> **Confirmation questions ensure that you're headed in the right direction. More importantly, they give the customer confidence that you understand their situation.**

Up to this point, we've covered a new way of structuring the discovery process. The goal? To maximize your understanding of the clients' mission to improve their lives. Now, the question is: What do we do with it?

It's one thing to have great information; it's another to be able to leverage it properly. But that's precisely what separates the real pros from the amateurs.

Here's what usually happens with a book like this: The majority of salespeople will cherry-pick the parts they like from what they've read so far and attempt to apply it. A small minority will embrace the four discovery categories and use them as part of their sales technique. However, it's in the summary questions where a select few will stand apart. They'll be the ones who use this tool to its fullest potential.

I want to suggest that the summary questions I'll show you have the potential to completely revolutionize your sales presentation. They're exceedingly powerful questions that will take your sales game to an entirely new level. More important—and I assure you this happens if you do it properly—*your clients will love you for it!*

The technique is comprised of two questions that come directly after your four Discovery Categories (hence the 4:2 Formula). You can't do the "2" without the "4." You have to get the Discovery Categories down first. Without those, you have only half of the story; it's like trying to put a roof on a house when you haven't built the walls yet.

I call these "Vision Agreement Questions." They summarize everything I've learned from the clients thus far in the process. They recap their experience, pain, fear, hopes, and dreams, succinctly and effectively.

The Vision Agreement Questions start with a clear understanding of the clients' mission. Remember, they're on a mission to improve their lives. They want their kids to be safe. They want friendly neighbors. They want a home they're not embarrassed to show to their friends and coworkers. They want the freedom, flexibility, and peace of mind that comes with whatever their Future Promise holds for them.

They want you to show them how their lives will improve.

> **The Vision Agreement Questions start with a clear understanding of the clients' mission.**

When I've discovered the clients' mission, it's time to rephrase that back to them in the form of closing agreement questions. You see, I want the clients to agree—not with me, **but with themselves**. The clients need to acknowledge internally how their lives will improve.

The Vision Agreement Questions do just that.

The Vision Agreements

These two questions (the "2" of the "4:2") make for a powerful summation of the conversation at this point, and they direct the remainder of the sales process.

There are two Vision Agreement Questions:

1. The Summary Dissatisfaction Question

2. The Summary Solution Question

There are three compelling advantages to using the Vision Agreement Questions:

1. They bring clarity of thought to your clients, helping them to focus on what really matters.

2. They prove your commitment to understanding. As the salesperson, you're recounting what you've heard and confirming you heard correctly. Most salespeople never do this, but you'll find it's most welcome and greatly appreciated by a client.

> *"One of the hardest questions to ask, if you don't know your buyer on a deeper level and haven't established a shared vision and mutual purpose, is the closing question. My team understands the significance of vision agreements and the impact it can have on their buyer's Emotional Altitude and providing the opportunity for buyers to envision themselves in that space. All those 'yeses' along the way build positive energy, increase their confidence in their sales presentation, and have a huge impact in closing the deal!"*
> —Ashlee Roeder, Area Sales Manager

3. They lock in place both the Current Dissatisfaction and the Future Promise and they demand an action response. The clients agree *with themselves* that action must be taken.

AMY O'CONNOR
Mastery Level Insights

There's no better compliment for a salesperson than for a customer to say, "That guy gets me," or, "She really understands what I'm going through." We all want to be understood. More importantly, we want others to confirm that they understand.

The Vision Agreements offer an opportunity to demonstrate respect. It's the sales professional's way of saying, "You matter. You matter enough that I'm willing to restate what you've told me to make sure I have this right."

But here we're not simply restating the facts; we're restating the emotions. We're not just rehashing Current Dissatisfaction and Future Promise. We're handing back to our customers their current pain and future joy.

Study Questions

1. Why would clients appreciate the Vision Agreement process? What value does it add for them?

2. Why are clients more motivated to take action after the Vision Agreement process?

Chapter Twenty

Summary Question #1: The Summary Dissatisfaction Question (SDQ)

Step One: Recap the Pain

The first of the Vision Agreement Questions is called the "Summary Dissatisfaction Question," and the name fits quite well. With this question, I recap the clients' pain and confirm why change is necessary. For example, I can say to them:

> *"Let me make sure I'm clear—if you stay where you are, you'll be living in a home that you've clearly outgrown, your children will be in a school you're not thrilled about, and your maintenance bills will continue to increase. Do I have that right?"*

Let me break that down.

> **The Summary Dissatisfaction Question rephrases all that's wrong with the clients' current situation. It recaps their mission—how their lives need to improve.**

I simply recalled what I had learned from the discovery phase and fed it back in simple language. I'm not making anything up, and I'm not embellishing. I'm simply paraphrasing what the clients told me and repeating it back to them. This shows them I've been actively listening. If I did my homework and asked for the "why behind the why," I understand the problem in emotional terms. This technique simply recounts that; it confirms to the clients that staying put is not an option.

The structure of the question is as follows:

1. Begin the summary using the phrase, *"Let me make sure I'm clear on this…"* as a way to communicate that you're restating what you've learned. You don't have to say these exact words; choose the language that works best for you.

2. *"If you stay where you are…"* The key is to direct them back to what was wrong *before* they met you. It's not about what they miss out on if they don't move forward—it's about why they're in the market in the first place, about what needs to improve.

3. *"You'll have to put up with…"* I want my clients to feel the pain, discomfort, and distaste in staying put. I'm not trying to be manipulative here; after all, it was that very dissatisfaction that brought them to me in the first place. I'm just feeding back what's already inside.

Summary Question #1: The Summary Dissatisfaction Question (SDQ)

4. *(List the Items)* Simply list the key reasons why their current situation isn't right. Be careful not to phrase this in terms of what they'll miss out on if they don't move forward—that comes from the Summary Solution Question. (We'll get to that.)

5. *"Did I get that right?"* Remember, this is a CLOSING question. It's not enough to just state it. Clients have to *agree* with it! Also note that there's a hard stop here before I move to the SSQ. I need to see the clients' heads nod once or twice.

If you do your job right, you'll find that your clients will appreciate that you were listening and that you understand them.

Application Break

- Recall two clients to whom you recently sold a home. If you could go back in time and place yourself at that moment in the discovery process where you had adequately determined their dissatisfaction, how might you have asked this Summary Dissatisfaction Question? What would you have drawn out of their previous situation that proved the dissatisfaction to be sufficiently elevated?

- If you can learn to do this on the fly—inserting the question at the tail end of the discovery period—you'll find a tremendous connection with your clients. Moreover, you'll find the clients agreeing *with themselves* that their dissatisfaction is quite high.

Bonus Opportunity for Top Pros

At times, you'll find that your clients' dissatisfaction is extremely high—so high, in fact, that staying put is simply not an option.

For example, let's suppose that these prospects come into your sales office because of ongoing crime in the area where they live. Let's further suppose that there was a shooting yesterday on the next street over. This incident constituted a "last straw" moment for your prospects.

In a case when the dissatisfaction is sky-high, you don't actually need to ask a Summary Dissatisfaction Question. Rather, you can offer this in the form of an assumptive statement.

For example, *"Wow. That's really tough. So, it sounds like staying put just isn't an option for you, is it?"*

As soon as the clients agree that staying put isn't an option, they've also agreed that they're moving *somewhere*. More than half the sale is already made at that point.

Look for those opportunities to make the Summary Dissatisfaction Question more of an assumptive statement, especially when you suspect the dissatisfaction is extremely high.

> *"My recent obsession is the summary questions, especially the summary dissatisfaction and really digging deep into this with clients by structuring the questions in the perfect, most effective way. Perfecting this can really build trust and help you to understand your clients' needs better. If you truly feel empathy for this client's dissatisfaction, it can become the sales agent's 'why' also."*
> —Jacki Matthews, Vice President of Sales

JEREMIAH GORE
Mastery Level Insights

Sir Edmund Hillary is arguably the most well-known mountain climber in the world. In 1953, Hillary, along with his Sherpa guide Tenzing Norgay, became the first climbers to successfully summit Mount Everest, the highest peak in the world. This achievement was a historic moment in mountaineering, making Hillary a household name around the world. Hiking up a mountain requires effort, perseverance, and determination to reach the peak.

Similarly, a sales process requires dedication, communication, and persistence to close a deal. Both journeys can be rewarding, but they can also be challenging and exhausting. Just like turning around before reaching the peak of a mountain can leave a hiker feeling dissatisfied, leaving out the 2 of the 4:2 is like turning around before reaching the peak of the mountain. You have worked hard during the discovery to understand the buyer's mission. Skipping the Summary Dissatisfaction Question is much like seeing the mountaintop and falsely believing you're already there.

Study Questions

1. Recount the five elements of the Summary Dissatisfaction Question. Identify what could happen if you left out one of the steps? (Go through the five steps and identify the impact from each.)

2. Why is it important not to bring in some of the Future Promise information at this point?

3. How is the Summary Dissatisfaction Question a closing step?

Chapter Twenty-One

Summary Question #2: The Summary Solution Question (SSQ)

Step Two: Show the Future

Immediately after the Summary Dissatisfaction Question is asked and answered, we come right back with the Summary Solution Question. This is a recap of the most important things your clients are looking for, presented in an exciting, promising manner.

Note that the question is asked immediately after the clients have agreed to the Summary Dissatisfaction Question. Think "boom-boom" in your technique. The clients just solidified the pain in their own minds; now add the pleasure.

The question sounds like this:

> *"So, I need to find you something that offers a bedroom for each of your children PLUS a quiet office space, a drop-dead gorgeous kitchen, preferably with quartz countertops and stainless appliances, ample closet space in the master, and a spacious yard that will work for two large dogs—did I get that right?"*

Again, I'll break it down:

1. *"So, I need to show you something that offers..."* This is not the oft asked *"If I could show you..."* This is a promise you're making to them, not a commitment you're asking of them.

2. *"...quiet...drop-dead gorgeous...ample...spacious..."* You want to use descriptive words that speak elegantly about the ideal picture. Make it dramatic and lift the tone of your voice!

3. *"Did I get that right?"* Again, this is a *closing* question. You need to see the prospects' heads nod north and south! And when they do, they've confirmed the clarity in their own minds. You've painted the picture; now all you need to do is find that house!

As stated, the Summary Solution Question is not an "If I could, would you?" question, as is taught in many training formats. With all due respect to other trainers, I'm not a fan of this type of question. (That doesn't make me right, but bear with me while I present my case.) The "If I could, would you?" technique can be seen as manipulative by an increasingly skeptical prospect. With this approach I am, in effect, asking a client to make a commitment on a concept. ("*If* I could...")

Not only is that technique potentially dangerous; I'm not sure it's necessary. If your clients have already agreed with you on your questions, then they've closed themselves in advance anyway.

Think about it: All you have to do now is show them what you just agreed to show them. When you do that, they'll have already admitted that a) they can't stay where they are, and b) you have what they're looking for. What about that is *not* putting you in a position to close?

> **Application Break**
>
> This might be the most important application point of all. Practice the Vision Agreements over and over and over again. Practice with no interruption between the two questions. As soon as the client agrees with the Summary Dissatisfaction Question, immediately ask the Summary Solution Question. There can be no pause and no hesitation. Think "boom-boom" in how you ask.

The Holy Grail of Discovery: Mutual Purpose

When you've completed The 4:2 Formula, you're doing more than nailing down the discovery of your clients' Current Dissatisfaction. You will have reached the most coveted of positions—that of Trusted Advisor. Only a few minutes into the conversation, you will have achieved mutual purpose.

> **Mutual purpose is the end-all, the signal, that you're on the same team and striving for the same goal.**

Mutual purpose is the end-all, the signal, that you're on the same team and striving for the same goal. Most salespeople never reach this point with their clients. That's why they continually feel as if making a sale is like playing a tug-of-war. Mutual purpose involves positioning yourself as a Trusted Advisor. It's the surest sign you're on the same page with your clients.

Together you'll seek the solution, and you'll do so as partners. How great is that?

MARY BETH BERRY
Mastery Level Insights

Is there any better feeling in the world than to be understood? To connect with and talk with a good friend or a loved one who "gets you"? To feel validated in your opinions and emotions?

How do we know that the people in our life understand us? You can tell by the way they act—the way their emotions mirror ours; their sincere empathy; the way they listen.

How amazing would it be to bring this same feeling to your customers? To demonstrate to them that you "get" them? That's what you're doing with the "summary solution." It's so much more than a technique—it's a confirmation that you understand your customer's mission. How incredibly powerful do you think it is for your buyers to feel this level of understanding? When you repeat back your customers' wants and needs while painting a picture of what their future could feel like, you confirm that you understand them.

You'll know when you get this technique right because not only will you see your customer start to get excited, but YOU will also start to get excited. You're on a mission to the same destination! You get each other. That little spark of magic when you hear your customers say "Yes. That's what I'm looking for!" is called Mutual Purpose. It's the best feeling in the sales world—for your buyer…and for you!

Mutual purpose is the ultimate goal, but it requires several components to be in place, which we've already addressed, including:

- ✓ Rapport and trust; likability (coffee worthy)
- ✓ Understanding of Buyer's Motivation (on a deep level)
- ✓ Knowing the Current Dissatisfaction
- ✓ Knowing the Future Promise
- ✓ Summarizing the Dissatisfaction
- ✓ Summarizing the Solution

> *"Being able to put yourself in a customer's viewpoint while getting to know them on another level and use their words when presenting their options to them is so incredibly powerful. It not only builds trust with the customer but cultivates a relationship with your buyer that other salespeople most likely aren't creating, making you and your company their #1 choice for such a big life change."*
> —Kaylie Austin, Division Sales Manager

Study Questions

1. What are the three elements of the Summary Solution Question?

2. Have you ever felt that you've achieved mutual purpose with a client? How did you feel? What was different about that search and selling experience vs. others that were not close to achieving mutual purpose?

3. As review, list the six items in The 4:2 Formula. Did you get them all? Now memorize them!

Chapter Twenty-Two
Filling In the Information Gaps

> *"Ask small questions and you get small answers."*
> – Jeff Shore

If you've been paying close attention, you'll notice we missed a few minor details along the way, things like:

- Price Point
- Square Footage
- Time Frame
- Financing Capability
- Bedroom Count

Wow. Aren't these important things to have left out of a book that focuses on knowing your client? Stay with me; this will make perfect sense when I'm done.

By no means am I suggesting that the details in the checklist are not important; nothing could be further from the truth. Rather, the focus is on timing—that is, *when* is the right time to determine those things?

I contend that if you follow the 4:2 Formula, something amazing will happen. You'll learn those things without having to ask the questions! So often the "why" questions will lead you to the "what" answers.

Of course, it doesn't always happen that way, so you need to be prepared to ask some fill-in-the-gap questions after you've finished the 4:2 process. The key is in the technique. I propose a method of making those detail questions much easier for the client to answer.

> **Ask questions that are easy for your customer to answer.**

Suppose you walk into a car dealership. You had previously decided you would spend up to $30,000 for a new car. The salesperson approaches and immediately asks, "What is the most you're willing to spend?" If you're like most car buyers, you'll probably answer something like, "$27,500." Why would you give a bald-faced lie like that? Because it's a difficult question to answer. You'd fear that you were putting yourself at a disadvantage.

Now let's suppose the car salesperson asked about why you needed a car first and *then* about what you were looking for. Suppose the sales professional was mission-oriented and completely coffee worthy. Five minutes into the presentation, the salesperson says, "The car I want to show you offers (list of features) and it sells for $29,500. Is that in the price range you were hoping for?"

See the difference? In the second approach, the sales professional makes it much easier to answer the question. This is *exactly* the technique I suggest you use.

Here's how it works: Once you've learned what you need to know about the client's mission (using the four discovery categories) and established mutual purpose with the prospect (using the Vision Agreement Questions), complete this portion of the conversation by describing what you want to show them and asking if the details will work for them.

Instead of asking, *"How many bedrooms are you looking for?"* say, *"Based on what you've told me I have a home I definitely want to show you. It has four bedrooms and is about twenty-three hundred square feet. Is that what you were hoping to find?"*

Instead of asking their price point, say, *"The home is priced at $475,800. Does that sound like the price range you were hoping to find?"*

Instead of asking for their time frame, ask, *"We have a home that can be ready for move-in in sixty days, or we can build one for you in about seven months. Which of those time frames works best for you?"*

> "Mutual purpose is where the magic happens. After we have summarized the current dissatisfaction and future promise in a detailed way that has gained us trust the mutual purpose is where we can set all the expectations on pricing, what we can accommodate, things on their list we can't accommodate, delivery, home type, and home site expectations. If done right an agreement to the mutual purpose and to continue the process is essentially an agreement to purchase the home."
> —Frank Ryan, Community Sales Manager

Note that I'm only using this technique to fill in the gaps of missing information. If I did the 4:2 properly, I'd probably already know these things!

RYAN TAFT
Mastery Level Insights

If you've ever been to a restaurant, you've likely identified a predictable pattern in how servers take your order. They'll come up to the table, make a little small talk and at some point, ask you and your party for a small decision. It sounds like this: *"Hi there. My name is Brooke and I'll be your server tonight. What can I get you for appetizers and drinks?"*

Shortly after drinks and appetizers start appearing, Brooke comes back and asks: *"Alrighty...what can I get you all for dinner?"*

As the meal progresses, Brooke appears fairly close to the last few bites and throws a dessert menu at you, asking: *"What's it going to be for dessert?"*

I want to point out that Brooke didn't come to the table and ask this question: *"What would you like for apps, drinks, main course and dessert? GO!"*

She's giving your brain small, easy decisions to make. So, when filling in the gaps, be like Brooke. Confirm the following in three separate agreements:

- *Floor plan (appetizers and drinks)*
- *Time frame (main course)*
- *Price (dessert)*

To your customer, easy equals right!

> **Application Break**
>
> Practice *not* asking typical questions that are regularly asked in sales conversations (e.g., bedroom count; time frame; price point, etc.) during the first five minutes of the conversation. Just get to know the client using the 4:2 process and see if you don't learn all that you need anyway.

So, there you have it, The 4:2 Formula, the key to uncovering your clients' Current Dissatisfaction and delivering their Future Promise. There's no other sales method quite like it. But you have to be willing to apply it.

Now the real work begins. Don't just read—apply. Don't just take notes—practice. Lean into the opportunity to dramatically improve your presentation. Do this for your success. More than that, do this for your customer!

SECTION 4:

♦ ♦ ♦

Implementation

All right, my friends. You've made it this far. Now let's get this kicked into productive application. My job is to give you the education; your job is to use it in your sales environment. It doesn't matter what the consultant puts on the page; the only thing that counts is what you decide to put into action!

To get started, I'm making a strange recommendation. Please reread 10 segments of the book, this time at a much slower pace. Trust me, it'll be way easier the second time. But more important, the results will be dramatically more powerful. Here's why.

Not unlike music, drama, athletics, dance, or even surgery, sales is a performance art. How does one attain mastery in a performance art? Your instinctive answer is probably "practice," and you're partially correct. But as stated previously, it's *repetition* that makes the real difference. A dancer performs the same move over and over again. An athlete takes part in the same drill dozens of times in a row. And if I'm having surgery, I would prefer to be under the care of a surgeon who has more than a few notches on their surgical belt.

Every time we repeat a behavior properly, we find that competency to be more deeply ingrained into our subconscious. We make that behavior more automatic, more refined, and more polished. Moving toward unconscious competence comes only through repetition.

My challenge to you is to go back and read through 10 segments in 10 weeks, all while taking the lessons to an entirely new depth. I'll lay out that schedule for you here; your job is to commit to getting beyond "head" knowledge and build the repetitive mental muscle that locks the behavior deep into your psyche.

Three things will help you maximize this journey:

1. Be sure to journal throughout. Writing down your thoughts, progress, frustrations, questions, and so on will prove to be an invaluable effort. Journaling keeps you focused and allows you to measure your progress. There's a degree of self-accountability you'll experience by journaling. If you've never tried it, this is the perfect opportunity. We've given you plenty of space for that purpose in this book.

2. Find a practice partner. You can attempt to practice alone, but your progress will be dramatically improved by having a partner. Partners see things that you don't. They hold you accountable in your practice patterns. They can coach and encourage along the way. If you're looking to ramp up your performance more quickly, this is the way to do it.

3. Apply every day. You want to build in habits of constant performance improvement. This comes through daily practice and attention. If you leave the project aside even for a couple of days, you'll notice immediate consequences. First, your aptitude will decline quickly. Second, your motivation will recede, making it harder to start again. Third, you'll be hesitant to actually attempt the techniques in a sales conversation. So, make this a daily commitment.

The 10-Week Study Guide to 4:2 Selling

Week 1: Build Trust

- Reread Chapter 15 on relationship building.

- Make a list of the "coffee-worthy" attributes you wish to project. Share that list with others and solicit their input.

  Coffee-Worthy Attributes:

  _____

  _____

  _____

  _____

  _____

- Practice your most fully engaged, positive-energy greeting. Make a decision to stand out in an instant. Practice good facial posture. Be 100% present.

Elements of My Perfect Greeting:

_____

_____

_____

_____

- Pay attention to how your initial coffee-worthy attitude is paying off as you extend the discussion with your prospects. Journal the difference that your attitude makes in the remainder of the conversation. Celebrate the victory.

_____

_____

_____

_____

_____

- Build the habit of strong positive energy right out of the gate. Write down a positive habit-forming statement and read it before every sales encounter.

_____

_____

Week 2: Permission to Question

- Reread the section from Chapter 15 on the "Permission to Question" technique.

- Rewrite that question in your own words. Read it out loud several times to make sure it's exactly as you'd say it in an actual conversation. Make sure the question covers these three messages you're attempting to convey to your prospect:

    1. *"May I ..."* (you, client, are in control)

    2. *"...a few quick questions..."* (this won't take long)

    3. *"...point you in the right direction?"* (this is for you, not for me)

- Practice asking that question out loud over and over again. Get it down so it's natural and conversational. Remember, it's best to practice with a partner for added accountability and faster results.

- Use the question five times this week with clients. Check a box each time you use this question.

1	2	3	4	5

- Journal your progress. Write a brief statement on how you're doing so far. Celebrate your victories. Focus on progress each day.

_____

_____

_____

_____

_____

Week 3: Motivation

- Reread Chapter 16 on determining your prospects' motivation.

- Think back on the last three people you've sold a home to. Jot down *their* motivation, explaining how their lives needed to improve.

    1. _____

    _____

    _____

    2. _____

    _____

    _____

    3. _____

    _____

- Think through the most natural way to ask the motivation question, referring back to Chapter 16 for suggestions. Write out your ideal Motivation Question, saying it out loud as you go to make sure it sounds like you.

    _____

    _____

    _____

- Practice the motivation question over and over. Do this dozens of times over several days. Practice until the question is automatic and conversational, until you don't have to think about it when you ask.

- Once the Motivation Question is down solid, practice by beginning with the "Permission to Question" (lesson from Week 2) and immediately transition into the Motivation Question without a pause.

- Use the question five times this week with clients. Check a box each time you use it.

1	2	3	4	5

- Journal your results as you go along, paying particular attention to your comfort level in how you ask.

_____

_____

_____

_____

_____

Week 4: "Tell me more…"

- Reread Chapter 5, "The Why Behind the Why."

- Immediately begin to expand your curiosity skills by implementing this technique in your daily life. Use it in three non-sales conversations (either in your business life or in your personal or social life). Journal your results.

_____

_____

_____

_____

_____

- Practice making the "Motivation" and the "Tell me more…" questions seamless—that is, assume a "tell me more" follow-up with every motivation question.

- Intentionally practice this "Tell me more…" technique on the heels of your motivation question with three clients this week.

- Journal your progress in using all three components: 1) Permission to Question; 2) Motivation Question; 3) "Tell me more…"

_____

_____

_____

_____

_____

Week 5: Current Dissatisfaction

- Reread Chapter 17 on discovering Current Dissatisfaction.

- Think of the last home you purchased or rented. What was the dissatisfaction in this *previous* situation that spurred your move? Write it down.

    _____

    _____

    _____

- Think of three prospects you're working with today. List some aspects of their Current Dissatisfaction. Be sure you're stating these in emotional terms.

1. _____
   _____
   _____

2. _____
   _____
   _____

3. _____
   _____
   _____

- Write out your ideal Current Dissatisfaction question. As you write, say it out loud several times to ensure it's natural for your style.

   _____
   _____

- Use the exact Current Dissatisfaction question with three clients this week. Journal your efforts each time, adjusting to your greater effectiveness and celebrating your victories.

   _____
   _____

Week 6: Future Promise

- Reread Chapter 18 on determining Future Promise.

- Think of the home you live in right now. Based on your Current Dissatisfaction, what are some key elements of Future Promise in your next home? Write them down.

- Think of three prospects you're working with today. List a few aspects of their Future Promise. Pay special attention to the emotional aspects; share what you think will bring them joy.

1. _____

_____

_____

2. _____

_____

_____

3. _____

_____

_____

- Write out your ideal Future Promise question. As you write, say it out loud several times to ensure it's natural to your style.

_____

_____

_____

- Use the exact Future Promise question with three clients this week. Journal their responses and evaluate your effectiveness.

_____

_____

Week 7: Summary Dissatisfaction Question

- Reread Chapter 20, "The Summary Dissatisfaction Question."

- Think of the last people you sold a home to. If you were to rephrase their Current Dissatisfaction before you actually showed them a home, what would that question sound like? Be sure to follow the structure of a good Summary Dissatisfaction Question ("If you stay where you are, you'll have to put up with…Is that right?")

1. _____

2. _____

3. _____
   _____
   _____

- Think of three prospects you're working with today. Practice ways you could be asking the Summary Dissatisfaction question. Use this as a repetition process, repeating the question over and over and improving each time.

  1. _____
     _____
     _____

  2. _____
     _____
     _____

  3. _____
     _____
     _____

- Practice using the Summary Dissatisfaction Question three times this week. Journal your efforts each time, adjusting to your greater effectiveness and celebrating your victories.

_____

_____

_____

_____

_____

- Remember that this is an advanced technique, and, like any advanced technique, it takes time and repetition to perfect. Focus on your progress and celebrate every step.

Week 8: Summary Solution Question

- Reread Chapter 21, "The Summary Solution Question."

- Think of the last people you sold a home to. If you were to rephrase their Future Promise before you actually showed them a home, what would that question sound like? Be sure to follow the structure of a good Summary Solution Question ("So, I need to show you something that offers…Is that right?")

_____

_____

_____

- Think of three prospects you're working with today. Practice ways you could be asking the Summary Solution question. Use this as a repetition process, repeating the question over and over and improving each time.

    1. _____

    _____

    _____

    2. _____

    _____

    _____

    3. _____

    _____

    _____

- Practice using the Summary Solution Question three times this week. Journal your efforts each time, adjusting to your greater effectiveness and celebrating your victories.

_____

_____

_____

_____

_____

_____

Week 9: Filling in the Information Gaps

- Reread Chapter 22, "Filling in the Information Gaps."

- By now, you should be deferring on all those rote questions that everyone else asks right out of the gate (e.g., bedroom count, time frame, price range, etc.). If not, diligently force yourself to suspend those questions until after the 4:2 progression.

- Find a practice partner and go through the entire 4:2 progression at least three times. Ask the practice partner to come up with a different buyer profile each time. At the conclusion of each 4:2, use the techniques from Chapter 22 to fill in the information gap.

- Journal your results as you go.

Week 10: Celebrate Your Victory!

- Reread your journal notes going all the way back to Week 1 of your practice assignments. Celebrate the progress you've made along the way.

- Think back to your sales presentation before you started this journey. What are the three most significant changes in your approach, and how have they helped you become a better sales professional?

1. _____
   _____
   _____

2. _____
   _____
   _____

3. _____
   _____
   _____

- Read the stories of Ashley and Stephanie in the pages that follow. Based on what they say, how can you continue to improve your own performance going forward?

Appendix 1

Success Stories

Success Story #1: Ashley Hinesley, Nashville, TN

You're a veteran salesperson. How has your selling style changed over the years?

When I started in sales, I was taught to ask the same questions I still hear from other salespeople: bedroom count, price range, time frame, and so on. But then you find yourself suggesting floor plans that fit the answers to those questions when you don't fully understand what's most important to the clients. Today, the most valuable piece of information I can find out is their motivation. Why are they moving in the first place?

Then I have an in-depth conversation that goes much deeper into their lives than I used to go. But I've learned that knowing *why* they're moving leads to a better alignment between my clients and me. As a result, we get to the right solution more quickly.

Why is that true?

I have so many homes I could show to my clients, and if all I knew was their bedroom count and price range, it would take forever to show them all. Let's face it: If I only knew they wanted four bedrooms at a price below $250,000, I wouldn't have a sense of where to start.

Now, I look to show them something that relates to their lives. I find out about their life situation today, and it tells me what they're moving *from*. Knowing that gives me clarity on what they're moving *to*.

What is the secret to that deeper discovery?

It's about leveraging the relationship and getting to know my clients on a deeper level. People are surprised at how much I can learn on the front end of the conversation. It gives me insights I would never have otherwise. And it leads me to interesting conversations and important information.

Are people hesitant to open up?

No, not if they believe I really care about them. I don't jump into the sales questions right away like I used to. Having this initial rapport-building time is critical in letting them know I care about them as people, not just whether they're going to buy a home from me. After that point, it's not difficult to get them to open up.

How are you standing out from the competitors?

I think I'm more memorable because I just don't sound like every other salesperson. At least that's what my clients tell me. Other salespeople are busy talking about their products; they don't really get into talking about the prospect's life.

Exactly which technique allows you to learn more in your conversation than your competitors do?

These days, I make a living off of one phrase: "Tell me more about that." In the past, I've wanted to rush forward to the solution, but I've learned that pausing and staying on a topic is not a bad thing at all.

Salespeople want to talk more than they should; that was always an issue for me in the past. I rushed to get to the product discussion quickly. It's still something I have to remember, but I've trained myself to go deeper to gain understanding. It makes all the difference in the world.

Do you have an example of how you've used The 4:2 Formula with a recent homebuyer?

I was working with a couple who'd been referred by their daughter. This older couple was moving from New York; their daughter lives here in Nashville. The father didn't want to open up right away, but he eventually stated he'd had a heart attack brought about by stress, largely from living in New York. I also discovered that the daughter was pregnant with yet another grandchild, and he was tired of living so far away from his grandkids.

The point is that this purchase wasn't about the home or the price or the lot size. It was all about how the couple could improve their lives!

There's a story behind every single person. I can one hundred percent say I've sold a lot of homes by getting to know my clients well.

Success Story #2: Stephanie Sharon, Charleston, SC

How has your use of the 4:2 Formula changed the way you sell?

I've always believed in being sincere, and I've always had a desire to serve my clients. What I've learned through the 4:2 Formula is that I serve them best when I *know* them best. Now I spend a lot more time getting to know them on a deeper level.

I've always been a decent performer, but now I perform on a whole new plane. I've always had good client feedback surveys, but now the scores are off the charts. My sales have sky rocketed since before I learned The 4:2 Formula. And now my sales have increased by fifty percent.

What are some examples of how your presentation style has changed?

The biggest change is what I hear from clients and even from other salespeople. I'm selling homes to people on the first day I meet them. Other Realtors are stunned at how quickly I can get people on contract. The biggest impact has been on how well I get to know my clients.

Give me an example of that.

I had a very, very grumpy couple come in looking for a home. From the start, they didn't want to talk to me, not even a little bit. It was just conversation like "give me a price sheet and let me walk around." I recognized from what I've learned about the 4:2 Formula that this is a symptom of their situation. These people aren't mean; they're just stressed out.

It turns out they had just driven 14 hours from Michigan for this house-hunting trip. And why? Because they recently suffered the loss of both of their dogs. These dogs were family members to this couple. Without them, they simply didn't want to stay in their home anymore. Also, because of the cold weather, they couldn't walk their dogs half the year. They wanted that to change with any future pets.

This couple purchased on the first day I met them, and by the end of the deal, we were like family. They were wonderful people. I just met them when they were completely stressed out.

Are you seeing a shorter buying cycle now that you're using The 4:2 Formula?

It's dramatically shorter. Recently, a competitor came to me stunned that I had sold a couple a home on their first visit. The same people had told that salesperson they had a two-year time frame in mind. Bottom line, I get to know my clients more deeply and quickly than others do. That helps me solve their problems in a fraction of the time I could in the past.

How are you using the Summary Questions?

Those questions are absolutely essential to me. They prove to the clients that I've listened carefully, and that I really want to make sure I've gotten everything right. It's so powerful; they *love* it that I've listened.

I've found that the Summary Questions tie the pieces together. Asking them also gives my clients an opportunity to let me know if I missed something. It increases my efficiency so I can take them on the right path more quickly.

Do the Summary Questions increase your confidence?

Absolutely! Now I know I'm taking them to the right house right off the bat. I don't have to guess, and I don't have to show them a ton of homes. We get to the solution right away.

Do you have examples of what you learned using The 4:2 Formula?

Two examples come to mind. The first was a couple who said they were in no hurry. They showed no energy or urgency from the start. When I asked why they were moving, they said they were renting and wanted a change.

It took several different ways of my following up with "Tell me more about that" to get them to open up. Eventually, they told me their apartment was infested with cockroaches. Not only were they embarrassed about their living conditions, but they also felt like bad parents to their two-year-old.

When they came into my office, they were "just looking." They had no idea they could actually *buy* anything. But buy they did. The most amazing thing is that their telling me what was really going on gave me one of the best feelings ever. I knew immediately I was hearing things that are deep and personal to them—things they wouldn't share with just anyone.

Here's one other example that's personal to me. A dear friend's husband passed away last year. It was obviously a difficult time, particularly for my friend.

One thing she and her husband enjoyed about their place was the abundance of trees surrounding their home. So, when she was looking for a new home during this difficult time, she wanted to get away from living among lots of trees. She found the idea depressing; it was a constant reminder of a life she could no longer have. But what do you think most salespeople talked about? Trees! They wanted to show her homesites with trees everywhere because they never bothered to discover her real issues.

That is really powerful. Any advice for new salespeople?

Most salespeople want to talk about the product. My advice is to get to know the people. You'll successfully determine the right product when you understand the people.

Appendix 2

Sample Scripts

As you read through these sample scripts, look for the 4:2 pattern in the conversations. By now, you'll have a good understanding how the progression unfolds. It might be helpful to read the salesperson's lines out loud to get additional practice honing your delivery.

The 4:2 Formula Sample Script #1

(SP = Salesperson; C = Client)

SP: Good afternoon. I'm Robert. And you are?
C: Wayne and Marianne. How are you?
SP: Doing great. Thanks for asking. How's your day going?
C: It's fine. A little tiring, but we're getting by.
SP: House hunting can be tiring, no doubt. But do you enjoy the process?
C: I guess. It gets confusing after a while, but we're hanging in there.
SP: Absolutely. Well, thanks for stopping by here. I know you have a lot of choices on where you could have stopped.

	Thanks for including us on that list. Can I get you a bottled water?
C:	We're fine, thanks.
SP:	Well, I want to be able to point you in the right direction. Can I ask you a few quick questions?
C:	Sure.
SP:	Great. Let's start here: Why are you thinking about moving in the first place?
C:	Our place is way too small.
SP:	Tell me more about that. What makes it way too small.
C:	We have three boys ages ten, twelve, and fifteen. They're very active and always fighting. And I work out of my house, so it's just not a peaceful environment.
SP:	So, you need not only more space but a separation of space as well?
C:	Yeah, that sounds right.
SP:	Tell me about the home. What isn't working?
C:	For one thing, it's only three bedrooms so two of the boys have to double up. Plus, my office is in my master bedroom.
SP:	And I take it that's not working out so well?
C:	Especially when I have to make calls to a different time zone.
SP:	Got it. What else would you like to improve?
C:	The kitchen is old; it needs to be completely updated. It just screams 1980s. The backyard is a decent size, but we would like something bigger. The boys spend a lot of time in the yard. Also, the utility bills are ridiculously high due to poor insulation. In the winter, we walk past the windows and can feel the cold breeze.

SP: That's extremely helpful. Thanks. Now, what are some of the "must-have" items on your list?

C: A great kitchen with an island and all the things that modern kitchens come with: granite countertops, stainless steel, lots of cabinet space, an island…

SP: Okay. What else is on the list?

C: Well, we'd love to have a bonus room that's removed from the main living areas—a place where the boys can make all the noise they want. And it would be great if we could find a three-car garage.

SP: Tell me more about that.

C: We're at that age when the boys will be driving soon, and we're going to run out of space to park our cars.

SP: Anything else you're looking for?

C: We'd love to have a really nice main bathroom.

SP: What do you have now?

C: A coat closet with a toilet in it! Seriously, it's really small and outdated.

SP: Thanks for sharing all that with me. Let me see if I've got this straight. It sounds like if you stay where you're at, you'll be in a home that you've clearly outgrown, with three active boys who are making for a less-than-peaceful environment, a kitchen you're not particularly proud of, and a primary bathroom that sounds like something from your first apartment. Did I get that right?

C: You nailed it.

SP: So, staying put just isn't an option for you?

C: That's correct.

SP: Got it. So, I need to show you something that complements your family in the way you live today. A great family room area that opens to the kitchen so you can be together when you want to be, but it has to have separate spaces for everyone; your own office tucked away from the common space; bedrooms for each of the boys; and a bonus room for the boys to escape to. And we want to see those great appointments that make a home so special: a drop-dead gorgeous kitchen with a large island and plenty of countertop space and a main bathroom you might find in a million-dollar home. Finally, you need a yard space that's big enough to let your boys be boys and a three-car garage. Did I get all that right?

C: That is absolutely right. We'd love to find exactly that.

SP: Good news. I have something I definitely want to show you. The home is five bedrooms and has twenty-eight hundred square feet. Does that sound about right?

C: That'll work.

SP: The home is priced at $655,500. Does that meet your price range?

C: It's more than we wanted to spend, but we're willing to look at it.

SP: That home will be ready for move-in in ninety days. How does that work for your timing?

C: We're renting our home now, so we're flexible.

SP: Outstanding! Sounds like we've got a real possibility. Let's take a look!

The 4:2 Formula Sample Script #2

SP: Hi, there! How are you?
C: I'm good. Thanks.
SP: I'm Marcia.
C: My name is Cindy.

SP: Hi, Cindy. You're out doing some home shopping—are you enjoying that?

C: It's fine. I'm a little rushed, but I'm getting through it all.

SP: Well, I can help you keep this as simple as possible. Can I ask you a few quick questions so I can point you in the right direction?

C: Certainly.

SP: Let's start here. What has you thinking it might be time to move?

C: I'm being relocated here from Denver.

SP: Oh, I see. How are you feeling about that? Excited? Scared?

C: A little of both. I was born and raised in Denver, so it'll be hard to leave. But the job is right, and I'm looking forward to a new chapter in my life.

SP: That's wonderful, Cindy. Congratulations. Tell me about the home you're living in now. What do you like about it, and what do you *not* like?

C: I'm in a townhouse now and I really like it, except for the shared walls.

SP: Tell me more. What is it that concerns you?

C: I don't want to have to worry about playing my music too loud or about a fire starting in one unit and moving to another. And I'm just ready to have my own space.

SP: Got it. And what are some of the important aspects of your new home? What's on your wish list?

C: I need a big kitchen.

SP: Tell me more about that.

C: I love to cook, so I need a lot of countertop space for preparation. I also plan to entertain so I want to have a gathering place in the kitchen—an island.

SP: Do you have a big kitchen now?
C: I do, and I love it.
SP: OK. What else is important to you?
C: I play the piano, and I need space for that.
SP: That's awesome. I wish I played. How big is the piano, and how much space do you need?
C: It's a baby grand. Right now, it's in my formal dining space.
SP: And is that working out for you?
C: Yes, it's perfect.
SP: Okay, let me make sure I'm clear on this. This job relocation is a sure deal so staying put is not an option. You *are* moving, right?
C: Right.
SP: So, to make this all work for you, we need to find the best of what you already have and combine it with what's lacking. That means a magazine-quality gourmet kitchen with all the bells and whistles; a detached home with your own yard and no neighbors to worry about; a defined space for your baby grand piano; and how about we include a main suite with a separate sitting area and a soaking tub in the bathroom?
C: That sounds perfect!
SP: I definitely have a couple of homes in mind. One in particular I think you're going to love. It's a three-bedroom home with a dramatic great room and a huge kitchen, and it's about eighteen hundred square feet. Sound good so far?
C: That sounds right to me.
SP: The home is basically ready for move-in today. Does that work?
C: The sooner the better.

SP: The home is priced at $479,900. Does that fit your price range?
C: Ouch. That's more than I was hoping to spend. Will the seller come down at all?
SP: Let me ask you this. Are we in the ballpark?
C: Yes, but it's just more than I had in mind.
SP: Fair enough. Let's take a look and see if you like it. If you don't like it, the price doesn't matter. But if you love it, then we can discuss the terms. Sound good to you?
C: Let's do it!